"Liz Curtis Higgs does it again—a touching, beautiful look at one of the Bible's most captivating women. This is a stunning blend of research, insight, and practical application that will challenge you and fill you with hope. You won't see the queen of Sheba or yourself in the same way again. Highly recommended."

—MARGARET FEINBERG, author of *Fight Back with Joy*

"Liz has the wonderful gift of making biblical history come to life. By the time I finished reading this fantastic book, I felt as if I knew the queen of Sheba. If you long to live, love, and finish well, you will treasure this book!"

—SHEILA WALSH, author of *Five Minutes with Jesus*

"Liz Curtis Higgs continues to knit our hearts with spectacular women in the Bible. In this treasure of a book, you will be captivated with the story of the queen of Sheba and how her all-out search for wisdom led her to the One of all wisdom. Thank you, Liz, for leading us into the riches of God's Word."

—LYSA TERKEURST, *New York Times* best-selling author of *The Best Yes* and president of Proverbs 31 Ministries

"Liz is someone who can hug you around the neck and still manage to kick you in the behind at the same time—my favorite kind of human. Prepare to laugh and cry and change."

—JENNIE ALLEN, visionary of IF:Gathering and author of *Restless*

"Liz Curtis Higgs is an expert at breaking down a Bible story and bringing it to life. Then she reaches out her hand and invites us to join her, right in the midst of the story, as she reveals the riches hidden there. Settle in with her words. Open your heart to the story. Find yourself on a journey of transformation and grace."

—DEIDRA RIGGS, author of *Every Little Thing*

"An unparalleled feast of rich truth, direly needed wisdom, and the most divine servings of grace. Every page sparkles not only with wit and warmth but with Liz's signature, unmatched insights. Liz is the comforting, courage-giving friend every woman prays for. There's no voice like Liz's. And there's no woman who can afford to miss the epic wisdom of the queen of Sheba."

—ANN VOSKAMP, *New York Times* best-selling author of *One Thousand Gifts* and *The Greatest Gift*

"In this stunning account of a woman that most people know very little about, Liz has masterfully (and responsibly) brought fresh insights to the story of the mysterious queen of Sheba. Her writing unites imagery and research in a seamless, spectacular way, and I learned many facts that breathed life into a few short passages of Scripture. I walked away from this book inspired to be more like the courageous, bold, wise, humble, and generous woman I met on the page. This might be Liz's best work yet."

—ANGIE SMITH, best-selling author of *Chasing God* and *What Women Fear*

Praise for
The Girl's Still Got It

"A perfect blend of humor, extensive research, descriptive language, and insightful commentary."

—*Publishers Weekly* Starred Review

"Liz writes with the mind of a scholar, the heart of a novelist, and a beautiful wit."

—ANGELA THOMAS, author of *Do You Think I'm Beautiful?*

"Her in-depth knowledge of the Scriptures, gifting as a communicator, and personal relationship with the Lord make her unmatched in ability to take biblical truth and make it applicable to anybody."

—PRISCILLA SHIRER, author of *The Resolution for Women*

It's
Good
to Be
Queen

It's Good to Be Queen

to Be

Queen

Becoming *as* Bold, Gracious, *and* Wise
as the Queen of Sheba

LIZ CURTIS HIGGS

WATERBROOK
PRESS

IT's GOOD TO BE QUEEN
PUBLISHED BY WATERBROOK PRESS
12265 Oracle Boulevard, Suite 200
Colorado Springs, Colorado 80921

All Scripture quotations, unless otherwise indicated, are taken from the Holy Bible, New International Version®, NIV®. Copyright © 1973, 1978, 1984, 2011 by Biblica Inc.™ Used by permission of Zondervan. All rights reserved worldwide. www.zondervan.com. For a list of the additional Bible versions that are quoted, see page 208.

Details in some anecdotes and stories have been changed to protect the identities of the persons involved.

Trade Paperback ISBN 978-1-4000-7003-9
eBook ISBN 978-0-307-45889-6

Copyright © 2015 by Liz Curtis Higgs

Cover design by Mark D. Ford; cover photos by Photononstop/Fabrice Lerouge, Getty Images/Daniel Bendjy

Published in the United States by WaterBrook Multnomah, an imprint of the Crown Publishing Group, a division of Penguin Random House LLC, New York.

WATERBROOK and its deer colophon are registered trademarks of Penguin Random House LLC.

Library of Congress Cataloging-in-Publication Data
Higgs, Liz Curtis.
    It's good to be queen : becoming as bold, gracious, and wise as the Queen of Sheba / Liz Curtis Higgs. — First Edition.
        pages cm
    Includes bibliographical references.
    ISBN 978-1-4000-7003-9 — ISBN 978-0-307-45889-6 (electronic) 1. Sheba, Queen of. 2. Christian women—Conduct of life. I. Title.
    BS580.S48H54 2015
    222'.5309—dc23

                                        2015013435

Printed in the United States of America
2015—First Edition

10 9 8 7 6 5 4 3 2 1

SPECIAL SALES
Most WaterBrook Multnomah books are available at special quantity discounts when purchased in bulk by corporations, organizations, and special-interest groups. Custom imprinting or excerpting can also be done to fit special needs. For information, please e-mail SpecialMarkets@WaterBrookMultnomah.com or call 1-800-603-7051.

To Rebecca Price
with gratitude, respect, and love.
From biblical Bad Girls to bonny heroines,
from the mountains of the Springs
to the glens of Scotland—
RP, you continue to be
a beautiful encourager and friend.

Contents

Great Sea

Memphis

Gulf of Aqaba

Sea
of
Reeds

EGYPT

ISRAEL

Jericho

Jerusalem

Hebron

Jordan River

Salt
Sea

MOAB

ARABIAN
DESERT

In the time of
Solomon and Sheba
10th Century BC

SHEBA

Ma'rib

Mocha

ETHIOPIA

Gulf of Aden

Arabian
Sea

*T*antalizing reports blow across the Arabian Desert like the fragrance of cinnamon on the night wind. One man's name is on every man's lips: *Solomon.*

He is indeed a king, but what is that to me? I am a queen in my own right, sovereign over the land of Sheba. I have lived long enough to know a crown means nothing unless the head wearing it is filled with wisdom and good judgment.

My traders tell me King Solomon of Israel is worthy of his throne. He rules his people with words rather than weapons. He surrounds himself with royal daughters from many countries. And when he speaks, his words are carved on clay tablets, then fired in the hottest oven, ensuring Solomon's wisdom will outlive him.

Travelers bring me his sayings, written on their hearts. I confess, the man intrigues me. How has he learned these truths? Who is his teacher? His father, David, was not only a warrior and a king; he was also a poet, a writer of many words. But Solomon's chroniclers say he surpasses David in wisdom.

I should be intimidated by this sovereign from the north.

Instead, the breadth of his knowledge inspires me.

A crescent moon hangs above my palace in Ma'rib as I smooth out a papyrus scroll. It is time I examined my own store of wisdom, plumbing the depths of all I have learned as queen.

Will my thoughts travel beyond the Sea of Reeds, as Solomon's have? None can say.

But if *you* choose to read them, that will more than suffice. And if I may test you with questions, so much the better.

Whenever we seek answers, we grow.

Sheba

One

It's Good to Be Bold

~~~~~~~~~

When the queen of Sheba heard about
the fame of Solomon and his relationship
to the LORD, she came to test Solomon
with hard questions.

1 KINGS 10:1

Queen Esther is easy to love. Queen Jezebel is easy to loathe. But the queen of Sheba? She wins my vote as one of the most fascinating rulers in biblical history—and one of the most infamous.

Anytime my mother wanted to put me in my place—let's say I was flouncing around the kitchen in some dime-store costume, wearing borrowed makeup, and putting on airs—she shot me a stern look, one eyebrow arched. "Who do you think you are? The queen of Sheba?"

If she meant to scold me, it didn't work. *Sorry, Mom.* Being the queen of Sheba sounded positively delicious. Having watched Gina Lollobrigida turn up the heat in MGM's *Solomon and Sheba,* I knew the score. Sheba was Delilah, Nefertiti, and Cleopatra all rolled into one—an exotic beauty from a foreign land with wealth, power, and sex appeal beyond anything this small-town girl could fathom.

Is that how you've imagined her too?

Then it's time to meet the *real* queen of Sheba.

A leader of uncommon boldness and vision, she traveled from the ends of the earth to seek wisdom. While many foreign princes visited Solomon, "no other ruler merits the same attention"[1] as Sheba does. Her search for truth is one of many reasons this ancient queen serves as a modern role model. True, at the start of things, she was a pagan queen, yet "she prized wisdom above power."[2] When a smart woman moves in the right direction, her steps inevitably lead to wisdom's Source.

As for her name, I found nearly a dozen possibilities. Ethiopians call her Makeda, meaning "greatness"; her Arab name is Bilqis; the Romans called her Nikaule; and her Jewish folklore name is Malkath, the Hebrew word for "queen of." Though *Sheba* is the name of her country rather than her given name, *Sheba* is how she's best known in Western culture today, so that's what we'll run with here.

Her story in Scripture is brief yet rich—a handful of verses in 1 Kings 10, repeated almost verbatim in 2 Chronicles 9. We'll stroll through her narrative phrase by phrase, marveling over the treasures to be found in God's Word.

The Lord doesn't speak in these passages, yet His name is rightly praised. Though no heavenly beings appear, we'll sense God's presence throughout. And while some may say there are no miracles in this story, I believe a changed heart is a wonder to behold.

Even King Solomon cleared his schedule to make room for the "very rich, very successful"[3] queen of Sheba. Suppose we welcome her into our busy lives as well and see what valuable lessons this Spice Girl of the Bible has to teach us.

LEGEND HAS IT

Over the centuries Sheba's story has been embellished by Jews, Christians, and Muslims alike. From chaste virgin to seductress, from goddess to she-devil, Sheba has become "whatever history wanted her to be."[4] What we're after is the Sheba of biblical history, the one who remained true to her royal calling.

By focusing on Scripture, we'll avoid the shadowy corridors of speculation and legend, lest we get distracted and lose our spiritual footing. "Her stories have been part of oral history for centuries. And in the telling, as with all folk legends, they sometimes become wildly embellished."[5]

In the Bible there's not a hint of sensationalism regarding Sheba, let alone any foundation for the scandals wrapped around her name.[6] Sexy Sheba lives only in Hollywood.

What can we know for certain about this queen of the desert? The things that truly matter: her words and actions, her motives and methods as recorded in Scripture. Together they reveal a woman almost as sage as Solomon himself. "Who is wise and understanding among you? Let them show it by their good life, by deeds done in the humility that comes from wisdom."[7]

Hmm. I thought being wise would make a person proud. God's Word says just the opposite. Genuine wisdom makes us genuinely humble. Sheba will show us how that works. Christina, queen of Sweden, once said, "Dignity is like a perfume; those who use it are scarcely conscious of it."[8] Humility is much the same and releases an even more beautiful scent.

An independent woman, Sheba was "at ease with herself and with her world,"[9] willing to venture far from home to quench her thirst for knowledge, wisdom, and truth. Though she was "educated with royal care, in all the learning of her country,"[10] Sheba was ever eager to learn more.

I'm sold on Sheba; I think you will be too.

Our camels are standing by.

TIME AND DATE STAMP

When the queen of Sheba . . . 1 Kings 10:1

Hold it. *When* exactly was "when"?

The First Book of Kings was compiled around 535 BC, but the material was taken from much older records and temple archives—likely from the time of King Solomon himself,[11] though even that timing is tricky to nail down.

Solomon isn't mentioned in any ancient Near Eastern resource other than Scripture, so we can't be sure how his reign lines up with other known historical events.[12] Most scholars peg his forty-year reign from 962 to 922 BC.[13] For Sheba's visit to Jerusalem, we'll circle 945 BC[14] on our calendars and call it done.

There's no mention of a king during her reign in the land of Sheba. An unmarried woman of royal blood, a virgin queen, Sheba was alone on the throne, although archaeologists have discovered evidence of several Sabean queens during this era.[15]

Suppose we take a spin around the country these women ruled.

LOCATION, LOCATION, LOCATION

The first-century Jewish historian Josephus called Sheba "queen of Egypt and Ethiopia,"[16] but most scholars today place her firmly in the country we now call Yemen, tucked in the southwest elbow of the Arabian Peninsula.[17] The word *yemen* in Arabic means "south."[18] Since Sheba is also known in Scripture as "the Queen of the South,"[19] we can look toward Yemen with confidence.

Modern Yemenites claim Sheba as their own and nod with approval when the daughters of their country are named Bilqis (Sheba's Arabian name) in her honor. And in the ancient inland capital of Ma'rib, where as many as twenty thousand people resided in Sheba's day,[20] archaeologists continue to explore sites that bear her name—the Throne of Bilqis and the Sacred Place of Bilqis.[21]

I've been to the Middle East but not to Yemen. Photos reveal a countryside of dramatic contrasts—lush vegetation in one area, desert in another. The rugged beauty of the landscape and the sand-colored buildings—often built to dizzying heights—help us picture the place Sheba called home.

Neatly wedged between the Near East and the Far East,[22] the land of Sheba was a paradise for exporters, enabling them to conduct sea trade with both Africa and India.[23] Her country produced some of the finest oranges, lemons, and apricots in the ancient world and delicious mocha coffee, named for the port city of Mocha on the Red Sea.[24] And the spices! Myrrh, balsam, frankincense, and cassia were so fragrant "the intoxicating scent of the blooms could be detected by voyagers offshore."[25]

Then one day reports began arriving from the north.

The Fame of His Name

. . . Sheba heard about the fame of Solomon . . . 1 Kings 10:1

A celebrity culture in the tenth century BC? You bet. What made Solomon so renowned? Not his late father, King David, or his title or his wealth or his massive building projects. It was Solomon's wisdom, "greater than the wisdom of all the people of the East, and greater than all the wisdom of Egypt."[26]

King Solomon was a bona fide rock star, "whose praise was sung by every passing caravan."[27] Without television or radio, newspapers or the Internet—with only traders on camels and sojourners on horseback—"his fame spread to all the surrounding nations."[28]

But it wasn't Solomon alone who commanded such respect. The world came to his doorstep because of Solomon's bond with the One who was wisdom itself.

. . . and his relationship to the LORD, . . . 1 Kings 10:1

When Sheba heard about Solomon, she heard about his God in the same breath. Solomon had clout because of "the reputation of the LORD" (EXB). Anything Solomon had going for him was "due to the LORD's name" (CEB).

The same is true for us, beloved. Whatever good we accomplish, the Lord is ultimately responsible, and He alone deserves the praise. The whole purpose of our lives is to magnify His fame and "sing the glory of his name."[29]

I know, I know—our culture teaches us just the opposite. We're supposed to magnify our own names. Collect friends like trading cards. Earn vast amounts of cash. Surround ourselves with creature comforts. Our spirits may wish to glorify the Lord, but our flesh has other ideas.

That's what makes Solomon a standout. From the moment of his birth, "the LORD loved him,"[30] and Solomon worshiped the Lord in return.

As for Sheba, in South Arabia of old, more than a hundred different deities were worshiped.[31] None of them was Solomon's God.

Did she hope to meet Him as well? Historic commentator Matthew Henry thought so, seeing her as "religiously inclined" and wanting to know more about the God of Israel.[32] If an earthly king could be so wise, imagine meeting the One who taught him!

ROAD TRIP

. . . she came . . . 1 Kings 10:1

Interesting that Sheba didn't send ambassadors on her behalf. The queen herself traveled a long way to see Solomon. Many others did the same. "From all nations people came to listen to Solomon's wisdom."[33]

We still do that. Women travel hundreds of miles to attend conferences, to hear and meet speakers, to be educated, encouraged, challenged. *Being there* is the thing. Experiencing it firsthand. That's what Sheba wanted too. "She was so interested, so disturbed, so curious, so hungry that she determined she would not depend upon the reports of others; she would investigate on her own."[34]

What sort of journey are we talking about? A long and tedious one. If you draw a straight line on a map, more than twelve hundred miles stretch north from Ma'rib to Jerusalem.[35] The actual route was probably closer to fifteen hundred miles, winding through the unforgiving Arabian Desert,[36] then across the land of Moab, past the Salt Sea, across the Jordan, through the fields and vineyards of Canaan, and finally climbing up to Jerusalem.[37]

Even the rocking motion of the camel—the "living ship of the desert"[38]— would've quickly grown old, not to mention the sheer boredom that inevitably sets in on a long trip. You know her servants must have whined, "Are we there yet?" In all, the journey would have taken more than two months,[39] since camels travel no faster than the walking speed of a man. *Groan.*

Sheba was clearly a bold adventuress—a "prototype and pioneer"[40]— who braved discomfort and thirst, bandits and thieves, sandstorms and scorching heat[41] as her caravan traversed the wide, trackless desert. Without warning a simoom—a dangerously hot, dust-laden wind known to sear across the Arabian Peninsula with violent speed—might have swept through their encampment. Fierce animals roamed the land as well—leopards, baboons, jackals, and hyenas—and deadly creatures like scorpions, cobras, and horned vipers.[42]

Queen Elizabeth the Queen Mother once said, "Danger is often overcome by those who nobly dare."[43] That's our bold Sheba: noble and daring.

Sheba and her entourage probably traveled in the winter, crossing the desert at night by torchlight to avoid the oppressive heat of day.[44] Every oasis brought a welcome respite of shade, cool water, and fresh dates. But after two long months, our road-weary Sheba was undoubtedly ready for the courts of Solomon.

TRADE SECRETS

She certainly wanted to ask questions and perhaps sharpen her leadership skills. But she also may have planned to negotiate a trade agreement with

Solomon before his fleet of ships put her old-school caravans out of business. In fact, some scholars are convinced the primary reason they met was to talk trade issues.[45] Solomon's new harbor in the Gulf of Aqaba, which allowed ships to cross from Arabia to Egypt, presented a serious threat to her spice trade.[46] As both a diplomat and a politician, Sheba knew a personal visit from a queen would accomplish far more than any ambassador could.

Whatever items topped her agenda, Sheba was bright, well educated, and socially adept. I'm telling you, the woman was impressive. Even so, "her greatest asset was a heart that desired wisdom."[47] Sheba had an insatiable hunger for knowledge, "a restless longing after the True, the Good, the Beautiful, the Eternal."[48]

Oh, to be described like that! Rather than longing for more power, more fame, more money, or more stuff, Sheba desired attributes that capture the essence of the Almighty: "The LORD is right and true,"[49] "the LORD is good,"[50] "He has made everything beautiful in its time,"[51] and "the eternal God is your refuge."[52]

True. Good. Beautiful. Eternal. That's what Sheba was searching for.

We want that too. In a world where lying is common, evil often triumphs, ugly deeds are celebrated, and people are satisfied with momentary pleasure, we need God's wisdom more than ever.

TESTING, TESTING

Sheba's journey began with a clever plan.

. . . to test Solomon . . . *1 Kings 10:1*

She wanted to see if this king lived up to all the hype. Her intent was to "challenge him" (NET), "try him" (DRA), "prove him" (ASV), and so "put his reputation to the test" (MSG).

It's been said, "Never engage in a battle of wits with an unarmed man." On that score Solomon was armed to the teeth. That's why Sheba's plan was so bold. She was "the first reigning queen on record who pitted her wits and wealth against those of a king."[53] Sheba was queen and she was confident. Plus, she knew what mattered most in life.

I once thought wealthy people chatted about their possessions: the mansions, the yachts, the furs, the jewelry, the fashions. Not necessarily. When I've had the chance to listen in on some of their conversations, here's what they've talked about: where they've traveled, what they've seen, whom they've met, and what they've learned.

That's real wealth, and they're sharp enough to know it. Being rich with material things isn't nearly as valuable as being rich with knowledge and experience.

Wisdom is "an ornament of grace to the soul,"[54] something money can't buy and skill can't earn. It does cost us something, though. Time. Effort. Focus. Sheba must have had those qualities in abundance. In her we see "a willingness to seek and sacrifice, to give whatever it takes to find answers to life's questions."[55]

So then, our bold Sheba prepared to test the king.

. . . with hard questions. 1 Kings 10:1

Josephus called them "questions of very great difficulty."[56] These "riddles" (CEB) and cryptic "enigmas" (YLT) had definite answers—if you possessed the wisdom to sort them out.

MIND GAMES

In Solomon's day such questions served as "a celebrated entertainment of the eastern princes,"[57] enjoyed at feasts and other special occasions.[58] To pick

apart the veiled meanings and allegorical language of enigmas required inge-
nuity and careful thinking.

I love word games—Scrabble, Boggle, Bananagrams—but I'm the worst
at solving riddles, puzzles, or games of logic. Sheba excelled in them. Apparently Solomon did too.

The book of Proverbs introduces its earthly author—"Solomon son of
David"[59]—who advised God's people to "listen and add to their learning,"[60]
specifically by "understanding proverbs and parables, the sayings and riddles
of the wise."[61]

Aha! *Riddles.* Solomon clearly loved and valued them.

Did Sheba know of his mastery in advance? Or did she discover his
superior skills after she reached Jerusalem? Since Arabic literature is filled
with riddles,[62] we can be certain Sheba was a talented opponent, coming up
with questions that "cloaked a deeper philosophical, practical, or theological
truth."[63]

Even though riddles often featured animals or plants,[64] they weren't
child's play. Instead, they were an opportunity for Sheba to display "her cun-
ning and statecraft."[65]

King Solomon claimed a single Source of wisdom: the God of Israel.
Sheba, a pagan queen with many deities, seemed determined to stump Solomon and his God. A risky move but nonetheless bold and completely in
character for this monarch.

IS BOLDNESS A GOOD THING?

Boldness is definitely good. Especially for anyone who seeks to please the
King of kings.

When the disciples prepared to share the gospel, they prayed, "Enable
your servants to speak your word with great boldness."[66] That can be our
prayer too—to share biblical truths with courage and confidence, unafraid

and unapologetic. God answered the disciples' prayer at once, "and they were all filled with the Holy Spirit and spoke the word of God boldly."[67]

Boldness is really about God, then, and not about us. Rather than a personality trait, it's an attribute of the Holy Spirit. If God resides in us and works through us, His love will pour from us like living water. He forgives our past, He empowers our present, and He holds our future in His mighty hands. "Therefore, since we have such a hope, we are very bold."[68]

BOLDNESS REDEFINED

Boldness doesn't mean having a big ego. Being arrogant, conceited, or self-centered. Acting in a forward, boastful, or pushy manner. As some of us have learned from experience, "When pride comes, then comes disgrace."[69] Let's not go there.

Boldness also doesn't mean being brash, careless, foolish, or reckless. As the proverb tells us, "He who hurries his footsteps errs."[70] Patience and practice are needed before we can speak with authority and act with assurance.

When I was in my early twenties, I desperately wanted to be a radio personality and so applied for a job at every station in a thirty-mile radius. I had an amateurish demo tape, a one-page résumé with lots of white space, and zero experience other than my ten-watt college radio station.

Yes, I was confident.

But I was also unprepared and woefully uninformed.

One job interview was particularly memorable. The station manager threw up his hands in exasperation. "You aren't even asking the right questions!"

Awkward? Oh baby.

I swallowed my pride, then said, "You've already invested a half hour of your busy day. Please take just five more minutes and tell me what I should be asking."

My honesty must have disarmed him. He spent another thirty minutes instructing me, coaching me, and helping me make the next interview more successful. You can be certain I did my homework before I knocked on another door (and got my first job in radio).

True boldness is God at work in us and often follows a long season of preparation. Doing research. Talking to people. Listening. Solomon rightly said, "The mind of the prudent acquires knowledge."[71] That means you and I need to find solid resources and trustworthy teachers to fill our heads and hearts.

If we read with discernment, the wisdom of the ages is within our grasp.

If we listen to sound teaching, we won't be misled by those who've been misled.

If we test what we learn, comparing it to scriptural truth, our foundation will be secure.

Still, facts don't make us bold. *Faith* makes us bold. If we believe what we've learned, it's because we trust the One who taught us.

Luke described how the apostle Paul went about his ministry: "He proclaimed the kingdom of God and taught about the Lord Jesus Christ—with all boldness and without hindrance!"[72] That's the kind of chutzpa we're talking about.

I Am Woman, Hear Me Roar

One of my favorite scenes in the movie *The Lord of the Rings: The Return of the King* is when Éowyn, a brave female warrior safely hidden behind her armor, faces the evil Nazgûl in battle. Looming over her, the Nazgûl growls, "You fool! No man can kill me."

Éowyn pulls off her helmet, releasing her mane of hair, then says through gritted teeth, "I am no man." (Audience cheers wildly.)

Many women sense boldness living inside them like a caged lion, pacing left to right, waiting for the door to open. Queen Elizabeth I confessed, "I am a lion's cub, and I have a lion's heart,"[73] and Solomon declared, "The righteous are as bold as a lion."[74]

What can we glean from the king of the beasts? When I asked our sisters online, they were quick to respond.

Louise said, "A lion is ever vigilant, ever watchful. Ears tuned in to every sound. Eyes that are all-encompassing. A nose that detects the slightest change in the air." In the same way, we need to use all our senses and check our surroundings before we speak and act. As Solomon wrote, "Ears that hear and eyes that see—the LORD has made them both."[75]

"Lions are regal in their bearing," Anne said. "They act like royalty and are treated as such." Sheba clearly understood this. A queen never forgets she's a queen. If we treat ourselves with respect, so will others. If we belittle ourselves, the world will do the same.

Cynthia said, "The lioness proudly and boldly stalks her prey." Could Solomon have pictured a female lion when he described the righteous as "bold as a lion"? Smaller, swifter, and more agile, the females do most of the hunting, joining with other females in their pride to stalk and bring home dinner.

The male lion protects and defends. The lioness provides. Both fearlessly do what God created them to do. Wouldn't it be wonderful if we could say the same?

Knowing our limitations can be even more valuable than knowing our strengths. As Karen pointed out, "A lioness doesn't waste energy chasing prey she can't outrun."

The key to boldness isn't merely *believing* God is with us or *trusting* God is with us; it's *knowing* God is with us. Not self-confidence, but God-confidence. Not "I have this," but "God has this."

Queen Victoria said, "We are not interested in the possibilities of defeat."[76] Neither are we, beloved. "For the LORD takes delight in his people; he crowns the humble with victory."[77] God gives us a different sort of crown from Sheba's gold one, but it shines far brighter. And it shines forever.

Surprised to find my brow damp, I motion to a nearby servant bearing a large palm frond. Ma'rib's heat is more stifling than usual, but I suspect my agitation comes from within.

As you can imagine, rulers travel to many palaces and meet many kings. But the prospect of this journey has consumed my every waking hour. The countless provisions! The mounds of trunks overflowing with gold and spices!

I am confident all will be in readiness but am less certain how we will be received. That is to say, how I will be received as queen. Some rulers do not welcome quick-witted females in their midst. Hence, I must temper my boldness with kindness and take care not to run roughshod over his pride. He is a king, after all, and worthy of my esteem.

Naturally, every woman in Ma'rib is begging to go.

I shall require the merry company of Tarub to amuse me en route. Makarim, who wears goodness like a crown, will serve me well in Jerusalem. Shadiyah wishes to sing in Solomon's courts, and Alimah is a skilled and graceful dancer. When the evening entertainment begins, their talents will bring glory to our homeland.

Whether or not the king finds me attractive matters little. I prefer to win his respect. Still, should King Solomon take note of my dark eyes or smooth cheeks, I have promised my advisors I will not object too loudly.

Sheba

Two

It's
Good
to Be
Open

Arriving at Jerusalem with a very great
caravan—with camels carrying spices, large
quantities of gold, and precious stones—
she came to Solomon and talked with him
about all that she had on her mind.

1 Kings 10:2

Sheba's hands were open, ready to pour out her store of riches. Her mind was open as well, eager to pour out her riddles and sayings. But when the Salt Sea came into view, what Sheba probably opened was her cosmetic case. Though she had much more to offer than her appearance, the Queen of the South needed to look her royal best before meeting Solomon the Wise.

What might she have looked like? When I asked two veteran missionaries to describe the people of Yemen, they spoke of deeply tanned or olive skin and dark brown, almost black hair, thick and full with loose curls. One scholar described their figures as "robust and elegant; their intelligence proportionate to that physical perfection."[1] And the Irish poet Thomas Moore wrote of the women of Yemen:

> Beautiful are the maids that glide
> On summer eve, through Yemen's dales.[2]

Even with those glowing reports, the biblical account doesn't call her beautiful or treat Sheba as a sex object. On canvas and on screen, she's often painted as a delectable dish, but God's Word doesn't go there, so we won't either.

What makes Sheba beautiful is the same thing that makes you beautiful. She was created in God's image and for God's pleasure with God's divine plan stamped on her heart. We have all kinds of lotions and potions to make us more attractive on the outside, but what's inside—our eternal soul—is all that matters to God.

Even so, our ancient sisters were all about beautifying the body, often traveling with chests holding two dozen or more granite jars full of ointments. (Good luck getting *that* past airport security.) Throughout Sheba's long journey, rich salves and unguents were likely rubbed into her skin as protection from the hot desert air.[3]

But her spa treatments didn't stop there. For royalty like Sheba, red ocher was ground and mixed with water, then brushed on their lips and cheeks, similar to modern lip gloss and blush. Kohl was applied with a small stick, drawn above and below the eyes. Then a single black line was extended from the corner of each eye toward the hairline, not unlike the markings of my tabby cats. Eyebrows were painted black as well—so dramatic! And their bodies were drenched in scented oils.[4]

Draped in the finest linens and silks and decorated with expensive jewels, the queen of Sheba was dressed to thrill as her camels began the steep climb toward Israel's capital.

YOU ARE HERE

Arriving at Jerusalem . . . *1 Kings 10:2*

Wait. Arriving? No details about the journey itself? No description of the endless hours of travel; the hundreds of camels, merchants, and servants; the petty arguments among Sheba's entourage; the difficulty in finding adequate fresh water; the dangers they faced? Not in Scripture. The Bible's focus—and ours—is Sheba's "quest for higher learning."[5]

Her long, winding caravan would have passed through neutral territories as well as hostile lands. Before her enemies could devise a scheme to apprehend her, Sheba and her treasures moved safely beyond reach, guarded by her soldiers[6] and carried by single-hump camels, able to plod across the desert a hundred miles at a time without water. At least sixty times her pavilion was pitched, and at least sixty times it was struck again before she reached her destination.[7]

Seated high above the ground in her elaborate litter with its linen curtains, Sheba escaped the blowing sand but not the intense heat or the ponderous gait of the dromedary. Anticipation must have thrummed inside her like the plucked strings of David's harp. Her questions were well rehearsed. Her gifts were meant to impress. Would she soon have Solomon eating from her hand? Or would the king quickly solve her riddles and send her on her way, making her wish she'd never come?

No. Her boldness had brought her this far. Her openness, her willingness to gain wisdom would carry her through Jerusalem's gates and into Solomon's presence. Was she nervous? Anxious? It seems more likely she shared the opinion of Queen Victoria, who said, "Great events make me quiet and calm; it is only trifles that irritate my nerves."[8]

We can imagine Sheba pushing aside the curtains, hoping to catch a glimpse of her destination. Two major trade routes crossed in Jerusalem.[9] The mix of cultures and languages would have been intoxicating for a woman like Sheba, who thrived on new experiences.

Built high on a ridge among the hills of Judea,[10] Jerusalem could be seen from miles away, in part because Solomon's temple, made of finely hewed stone and the cedars of Lebanon, "gleamed in the sunshine like a mountain of snow."[11] But Jerusalem wasn't the teeming urban center we know today. Surrounding the king's palace and temple stood a cluster of single-story houses, along with humble tents woven from goat's hair or sheep's wool. The population of the city during Solomon's time? Less than twelve hundred souls.[12]

Just as Sheba saw Jerusalem from a distance, so all of Jerusalem must have watched her approach. Messengers surely dashed about the city with reports as her caravan drew near. Her "grand and showy entrance" (MSG) into the capital must have created "an unforgettable spectacle"[13] and been "a great display of pomp" (NET).

But the staggering number of people accompanying her *really* had the city buzzing.

WE'RE WITH THE QUEEN

... with a very great caravan—... 1 Kings 10:2

How great was this company of hers? "Magnificent" (Knox) sums things up. The Hebrew word *chayil,* translated here as "caravan," means "strength, wealth, army." She brought "a huge entourage" (CEB), including advisors, assistants, and camels.

Why count animals along with people? Because a person's wealth was measured in part by the number of camels he or she claimed. Job, "the greatest man among all the people of the East," owned three thousand.[14] Our wealthy queen of the desert definitely had the camel angle covered.

The riches loaded onto those beasts of burden were even more jaw dropping.

... with camels carrying spices, ... 1 Kings 10:2

I'm picturing the spices in my kitchen cabinet, haphazardly stacked on a plastic lazy Susan. Not very giftworthy. Cumin seed, ground thyme, cream of tartar, red pepper, and a can of bay leaves stamped "Sell by March 19 11."

In all, my twenty little spice tins cost a grand total of sixty dollars, tops.

But the queen of Sheba put her spices on display first. Why? Arabian balm, native to her country, was perhaps "the most valued item in the whole inventory."[15] This special balm was used to ease pain, reduce anxiety, improve appetite, relieve indigestion, promote sleep—okay, we get the appeal. Sheba's camels "bearing sweet smelling things" (WYC) would have delighted Solomon, especially the myrrh, with its fragrant perfume, healing properties, and eye-popping price tag.

As the train of camels continued to pass through Jerusalem's gate, the crowd's attention shifted to more dazzling gifts.

GOLD DIGGER

... large quantities of gold, and precious stones— ... *1 Kings 10:2*

Sheba's numerous mines made her country one of the richest in the region,[16] producing "an immense quantity of gold" (DRA). Later in her story we're told precisely how much gold she left with Solomon: "four and one-half tons."[17]

Tons of gold. *Tons.* In today's money more than *200 million dollars.*

Wow. Need to sit down for a minute?

Now consider this: Solomon already knew these "riches" (DRA) would appear. When King David was dying, he dictated a psalm for Solomon, who would soon wear the crown. In Psalm 72, David prayed "May the kings of Sheba and Seba present him gifts"[18] and "May gold from Sheba be given him."[19] Whether they were prophetic words or simply the expectation of a king for his successor, both came to pass when the queen of Sheba showed up.

In George Frideric Handel's opera *Solomon,* the librettist wrote these words for our queen:

And now, illustrious prince, receive
Such tribute as my realm can give.[20]

Oh, quite the tribute! These "rare jewels" (Voice), these "stones of much worth" (NLV), included sapphires, rubies, emeralds, diamonds, and native agates in myriad colors—blue, white, green, gray, yellow, and red—cut and polished until they gleamed beneath the Arabian sun.[21]

Is it all too much for you? Too much to picture, too much to believe? Scholars assure us this over-the-top exchange of goods is "highly probable,"[22] although the thought of sojourning with such a treasure would make me a nervous wreck.

Now that she'd arrived, did Sheba simply wave her servants forward to present her riches, or did she place samples of each item in Solomon's waiting hands? Neither, it turns out. Gift exchanges came at the end of a visit.[23] By showing off her bounty at the start, Sheba assured Solomon that she'd not come begging but had brought sufficient riches to cover whatever expenses her stay in Jerusalem might incur. Rather like handing over your credit card when you check in to a hotel.

Wise as she was, Sheba also must have known that, when delivering an expensive gift, care must be taken, lest it land in the wrong hands.

Naturally, I learned this the hard way.

Gift Wrapped

Late one Friday evening a hotel clerk handed over my room key with the parting words, "Sleep tight!" When I slipped the key in the lock and the door opened only far enough for the chain to catch, I realized someone else was sleeping tight.

A distinctly male voice growled at me from the darkened interior. "Wrong room!"

"Sorry!" I pulled the door shut and checked the key. *Right number, right room.*

Confused, I sought out the friendly desk clerk, who scratched his head.

"I put a huge fruit basket in there for you too. A gift from your hostess. Had a gold box with *Godiva* on it."

Nobody gets my chocolate without a fight. Seconds later I knocked on the stranger's door. "Sir, that's my fruit basket you're holding hostage."

A hairy arm thrust out the pitiful remains: a sullied wicker basket brimming with gnawed apple cores, limp banana peels, and a box of empty confectionary papers. The note swinging from the handle read *Welcome, Liz.*

"But I'm Liz . . ."

"Then you're welcome!"

HELLO THERE

That would never have happened to Sheba's gifts. How can we be sure? She delivered them in person.

> . . . she came to Solomon . . . *1 Kings 10:2*

At last Sheba "appeared before" (CJB) the king and met him face to face. I wish I could tell you Solomon's exact age or describe how he looked. Neither the Bible nor history gives us those details. But we can sort out a few things from a careful reading of Scripture.

His parents were *fine.* When young David walked onto the scene, "he was glowing with health and had a fine appearance and handsome features."[24] Years later when David glimpsed Bathsheba, we're told "the woman was very beautiful."[25] Safe to say, Solomon had good genes from both sides of his family tree.

His birth was twice blessed. As the Bible tells us, "David comforted his wife Bathsheba, and he went to her and made love to her. She gave birth to a son, and they named him Solomon."[26] Born after the death of their first son, Solomon was deeply cherished by both his parents. Then "because the LORD loved him, he sent word through Nathan the prophet to name him Jedidiah."[27]

That's a lot to fit on a baby announcement, but every word is significant. His parents called him Solomon, from *shalom*, the Hebrew word for "peace" or "prosperity."[28] And God named him Jedidiah, meaning "loved by the Lord." Since in Scripture "a name is nothing less than a revelation,"[29] our boy was doubly favored.

His kingship was assured. "When King David was very old,"[30] he called Bathsheba into his chambers and affirmed his successor: "Solomon your son shall be king after me."[31] Overjoyed, Bathsheba prostrated herself before her husband and said, "May my lord King David live forever!"[32] He didn't, of course, but she was wise to honor her husband and secure the crown for her son.

He was a sharp dresser. A thousand years after Solomon's reign, people were still talking about his wardrobe. When Jesus spoke of the lilies of the field, He said, "I tell you, not even Solomon in all his splendor was dressed like one of these."[33] Solomon's clothing was evidence of his "wealth" (CEV), his "glory" (CJB), his "magnificence" (AMP).

It's almost certain that he wore a gold crown embedded with precious stones and placed on top of a cloth turban.[34] Solomon's robe, woven of fine linen and embroidered along the hem, reached to his calves or ankles.[35] And his flat leather sandals were surely fashioned from the best calfskin in Israel.

He knew something about women. To be specific, Solomon had "seven hundred wives of royal birth and three hundred concubines."[36] Oh my. A *thousand* women? We're told "Solomon held fast to them in love."[37] That he enjoyed the company of women is abundantly clear. That he understood them will soon be apparent.

We aren't told what happened right after Sheba's arrival, but common sense suggests a refreshing bath was in order, followed by a feast fit for a queen. The array of foods on Solomon's table would have included the finest Mediterranean favorites—olives and almonds, lentils and beans, figs and dates, pomegranates and melons, cheese and yogurt.

Still, no one travels fifteen hundred miles for a meal, however opulent. After she feasted royally, entertained by the court's skilled musicians, Sheba finally got down to business. This was why she'd come to Jerusalem. This was what mattered most.

TALK SHOW

. . . and talked with him . . . 1 Kings 10:2

After the description of tons of gold and heaps of frankincense, this long-awaited conversation seems . . . well, ordinary. Saying Sheba "communed" (ASV) with Solomon makes it sound a bit more personal, but, in truth, these two would have been surrounded by attendants—his and hers—trying desperately to listen in as she "asked" (ERV) her questions and "told" (Knox) the king what she wanted him to know.

Sheba not only sought wisdom. She also brought wisdom, including those fascinating riddles. I imagine she began with the most challenging of her brainteasers. They're not recorded in Scripture, but riddles attributed to her appear in other ancient sources, revealing "her vast knowledge of the world,"[38] from the history of the ruling families of Judah to this God whom Solomon worshiped.

Want some examples?

If she asked, "Who is he who neither was born nor has died?" Solomon would have correctly answered, "It is the Lord of the world, blessed be He."[39] Another riddle: "Alive, it does not move; when its head is cut off, it moves." Solomon would have known it was a boat in the water, made of wooden beams that were once living trees.[40] Or she might have posed the question

"What land is that which has but once seen the sun?" The wise king would have responded, "The bed of the Red Sea on the day when it was divided."[41]

It seems Sheba tackled a broad variety of subjects, from the natural to the supernatural. Did she really think she could best the king? Or did the two have a meeting of the minds, enjoying their point-counterpoint conversation, both rising to the challenge? Perhaps Solomon's own proverb flitted through his mind: "As iron sharpens iron, so one person sharpens another."[42] A man who is truly wise enjoys the company of a woman who can hold her own and keep his intellect engaged.

LEANING IN

Even the best of hosts can lose focus when a guest chatters on. Solomon, it seems, was willing to hear every word Sheba had to say.

. . . about all that she had on her mind. *1 Kings 10:2*

Not only what was in her head—those riddles, puzzles, and clever wordplays—but also "everything on her heart" (CJB). Sheba opened herself up to Solomon and trusted him with "all the things that she cared about" (MSG). They were strangers when they met. They knew *about* each other but didn't *know* each other. Yet Sheba "spoke intimately with him" (OJB). She bared her soul and confessed her thoughts, "emptying her heart to him" (MSG).

Such trust, such vulnerability.

What would compel Sheba to open up to this foreign king? Since they were equals in their roles, perhaps she felt safe with him, understood by him. Maybe the fact that he was a stranger loosened her tongue. An online sister named Tamara admitted, "I've always had perfect strangers approach me, talk to me, and ask me questions."

Jennifer has been there too. "I've been prompted by the Holy Spirit to pray with people I don't know—in public rest rooms, in a store, in the parking lot. I may be a little nervous about it, but I trust God and have never had anyone say no. I walk away in awe of His love and grace."

Sherry agrees. "When I share with strangers, it seems God placed them there just for me. Another example of how deeply God cares and how He is at work in our lives!"

In the same way, I believe the queen of Sheba's visit with Solomon was ordained and orchestrated by the Lord—primarily for Sheba's sake. Solomon himself wrote, "One who loves a pure heart and who speaks with grace will have the king for a friend."[43] Sheba's new relationship with Solomon was preparing her for a new relationship with his God.

Thrilling to watch, isn't it?

IN SEARCH OF TRUTH

Solomon was surely aware of God at work. Why else would a busy sovereign keep listening, keep encouraging her—verbally or implicitly—to share "everything she wanted to know" (NIrv) and "all that was in her heart" (NASB)? Solomon was a man who loved God, and he "showed his love for the LORD by walking according to the instructions given him by his father David."[44]

When this curious queen appeared with her bold questions and her open mind, Solomon must have realized Sheba was searching for more than just answers. She wanted to know the Source. As Queen Elizabeth I said, "There is one thing higher than Royalty: and that is religion, which causes us to leave the world, and seek God."[45]

Our spiritual journey often begins the same way. We talk to people. Ask questions. Try to sort out truth from untruth. We might speak with friends who have a walk of faith, though in the early days, that can be scary. *What if they treat me like a project? What if I make a fool of myself?*

So, like Sheba, we may prefer to open up to a stranger. We might not fully understand that it's God we're seeking and God who is listening. We just know we feel safe with this person who doesn't know us but meets our gaze and nods in the right places.

What Openness Means

The psalmist prayed to the Lord, "Open my eyes."[46] Jeremiah told the people of God, "Open your ears to the words of his mouth."[47] Paul urged the early church, "Open wide your hearts also."[48] Openness prepares the way for His Word to be planted inside us and take root.

Yes, it's possible to be too open. To be naive or gullible, to stand emotionally unprotected in the company of those who don't have our best interests at heart. Discernment is needed. But for most of us, the greater danger is being closed minded instead of open hearted, staying home rather than venturing forth, playing it safe instead of taking a risk.

How do we know if we're open to the Lord? Consider these three questions:

Am I willing? Can we accept what He tells us in His Word without arguing or resisting? James cautions, "You must believe and not doubt, because the one who doubts is like a wave of the sea, blown and tossed by the wind."[49] I spent enough windswept years in an ocean of doubt to know I am not going there again. Believing and then trusting are the first steps to being willing.

Am I eager? More than simply willing, are we *all in*? Is our greatest joy found in knowing and serving the Lord? Peter reminds us, "Who is going to harm you if you are eager to do good?"[50] Do our hearts sing at the thought of ministering in His name? Are we one of the first to raise our hands when volunteers are needed? Lukewarm isn't what the Lord is looking for. He wants those whose hearts are "eager to serve."[51]

Am I available? Do we have room on our calendars to go where God leads and do what God asks? As women, we often talk about not having enough margin in our lives. If we look at how we spend our waking hours, we usually find we've filled them to the brim. Yet David told Solomon to serve God with "wholehearted devotion."[52] That means putting Him *first* on our list, making room for Him not only in our hearts but also on our calendars.

Sheba was all of the above: willing, eager, and available. She proved it by traveling a great distance in search of divine wisdom and bravely placing her kingdom in others' hands.

She came to ask. She came to listen. She came to learn. Her eyes and ears, her mind and heart—all were wide open for King Solomon to fill.

Our King of kings asks us to do the same with Him. To be willing, eager, and available. To say yes when others might hold back. To be open to His teaching and open to His leading. To gladly trade everything we have for everything He offers us.

The truth? I'm not all the way there. As the apostle Paul writes, "Not that I have already obtained all this, or have already arrived at my goal."[53] So right. Some days I can't even see my goal. But I can "press on to take hold of that for which Christ Jesus took hold of me."[54] You can too, beloved.

Twenty years ago God called me to speak only for His daughters, leaving behind a decade-long career spent addressing male and female audiences in the business world. My speaking friends thought I'd lost my marbles. But I knew I'd found my true mission: encouraging my sisters in Christ.

The queen of Sheba shows us what happens when we open our hearts to something bigger than ourselves.

Torchlight bathes his gilded throne as I lift my chin, determined to meet the king's gaze before bowing with the others in my company. I study the sun-burnished face beneath his crown as long as propriety allows. His every feature is prominent. Brow, nose, mouth, chin. Yet nothing commands my attention like his eyes.

It is not the color of them. Olive green, golden brown, black as kohl— what does it matter? Light is what I am looking for. That unmistakable spark of intelligence and curiosity, brighter than any oil lamp.

There. I press my lips tighter, lest I smile and mislead him. He must see me as a queen, not as a future conquest. An equal seeking wisdom. Nothing more.

The noisy crowd pressing around the throne falls silent when my name is announced. I bow, taking care to keep my massive crown firmly in place. Then I rise to find Solomon studying me closely. This man collects wives the way some men collect knives, polishing them with care, displaying them with pride.

But Solomon does not look at me that way. His expression is open, welcoming, even kind. He holds out his gold scepter, a king beckoning a queen. I slowly ascend the steps, then touch the tip of it.

At once I feel lightheaded. Strange. Two words beat inside me, in rhythm with my heart. *Trust him.*

Sheba

Three

It's Good to Seek Wise Counsel

Solomon answered all her questions; nothing was too hard for the king to explain to her.

1 KINGS 10:3

I magine having *all* your questions answered by one person, complete with detailed explanations. Like Google with skin on.

But Google can serve up only the collective knowledge of humankind. Solomon shared wisdom from on high. "There was a divine sentence in the lips of this king,"[1] and when he spoke, Sheba listened.

Role model that she is, Sheba didn't solicit just anyone's advice. She consulted the wisest, most devout person in the ancient world.

So, I'm curious: Did these two chat for days? Weeks? The Bible doesn't offer any clues about how long Sheba remained in Jerusalem. Did she arrive in the month of Ziv? Depart in the month of Bul? Camels required at least two months to recover from such a strenuous trek, so we can be certain she tarried in Jerusalem at least as long as she'd journeyed.

Providing hospitality for her large retinue would have barely dented Solomon's treasury, especially considering the golden reimbursement Sheba brought with her. Besides, he needed plenty of time to show off his building projects—first and foremost, the place where almighty God promised to dwell among His people. A thousand years later Luke recorded "it was Solomon who built a house for him."[2]

IF YOU BUILD IT,
HE WILL COME

Construction of the temple began in the fourth year of Solomon's reign.[3] The portico with its two great pillars—named Jakin and Boaz—faced east toward the rising sun.[4] Ninety feet long, thirty feet wide, and forty-five feet high,[5] Solomon's temple wasn't enormous. The dimensions of the Parthenon were almost three times greater. But the temple was impeccably built according to God's design.

The walls were expertly hewed blocks of stone, polished smooth on their inner and outer faces. High, narrow, latticed windows kept the air circulating. The columns and roof were made of the finest cedar from Lebanon. The same wood lined the interior walls, such that no stone was visible, and planks of juniper covered the floors.

Carved into the wooden walls were gourds and open flowers, cherubim and palm trees. Inside the Most Holy Place, pure gold adorned the walls as well as two olive-wood cherubim, which stood fifteen feet high with their wingtips touching in the center of the room.[6]

Breathtaking just to picture it.

Everything was of the highest quality, from materials to workmanship. Solomon meant to honor both his father and the One they loved, carrying out the plans God had given David for the temple.

As a woman and a pagan, Sheba wouldn't have been permitted to tour the interior. For that matter, only the high priest stepped into the Most Holy Place and only once a year.[7] You can be sure Sheba thoroughly studied the outside of the temple, imagining the treasures hidden within.

Solomon's palace, built of the same hewed stone and fine cedar,[8] was completed by the time of her arrival, so that's where Sheba would have met with him to ask her questions and satisfy her curiosity—and surely his own as well.

LOOK WHO'S TALKING

Solomon answered . . . *1 Kings 10:3*

Solomon would have won every week on *Jeopardy!* because this man knew all the right answers. The Hebrew word translated "answered" here means "to be conspicuous," giving us a clear picture of this scene: Solomon was large and in charge. He firmly "told her" (ASV) and boldly "declareth to her" (YLT), sounding like Wisdom incarnate: "Listen, for I have trustworthy things to say; I open my lips to speak what is right."[9]

Not once in the biblical account does Solomon say "I don't know" or "Let me check with my advisors" or "I'll get back to you on that." Solomon had an answer for everything.

. . . all her questions; . . . *1 Kings 10:3*

Remember, Sheba came loaded with queries that boggled the mind. This particular Hebrew word for "questions" appears only twice in Scripture, in the two accounts of Sheba's visit. It specifically means *her* questions, *her* words. "Her matters" (YLT). Her questions were drawn from the deep well of her heart and cultivated in the fertile soil of her mind. Sheba was, in every way, an original.

Whatever she dished out, Solomon served back to her on a gold platter, providing answers to all her inquiries, "whether natural, moral, political, or divine."[10]

Solomon was not only bright; he was speedy. Despite all the "curious questions she propounded to him, he resolved them sooner than anybody could have expected."[11] But God, who knit Solomon in Bathsheba's womb and loved the child before he took his first breath, expected nothing less from His chosen king.

IF HE ONLY HAD A BRAIN

How did Solomon amass such wisdom? He asked for it.

When Solomon was at Gibeon, the Lord appeared to him in a dream and said, "Ask for whatever you want me to give you."[12] This wasn't a genie agreeing to grant three wishes. This was the God of the universe saying to Solomon, "Tell me what I should give you" (CJB).

What would you have asked for? A dozen healthy, happy children? A vacation home in Maui? A million dollars to invest in your favorite mission project?

I'm embarrassed to admit wisdom might not have made my top five.

That's why Solomon's response is so admirable. He began by praising the Lord's kindness to David in providing "a son to sit on his throne this very day."[13] Then Solomon humbly confessed, "I am only a little child and do not know how to carry out my duties."[14] He wasn't a preschooler—just untried politically,[15] a mere lad "in wisdom and experience" (AMP), who didn't "know how to go out or come in" (NKJV).

So Solomon asked of the Lord, "Give your servant a discerning heart to govern your people and to distinguish between right and wrong."[16] The perfect prayer for anyone in leadership: to make wise decisions with the heart *and* the head and to serve as a moral compass fixed on true north.

Naturally, the Lord was pleased with Solomon's request since the young king might have asked for a long life, vast riches, or victory in battle. God vowed, "I will do what you have asked,"[17] then also gave Solomon what he hadn't asked for—wealth and honor—"so that in your lifetime you will have no equal among kings."[18]

In true Hollywood fashion, Solomon woke up and realized he'd been dreaming. Does that mean his conversation with the Lord didn't happen? Not for a minute. God used dreams to communicate with Jacob.[19] And God said of His prophets, "I speak to them in dreams."[20]

Solomon knew his dream was the real deal.

Did he *feel* different when God gave him "a breadth of understanding as measureless as the sand on the seashore"?[21] Were there perceptible changes taking place inside his mind? A sudden sense of clarity? An awareness of new ideas, of expanded thinking?

This much we know: Solomon wasn't wise because he had a big brain. Solomon was wise because he had a big God.

ASK AND SEEK

We worship and serve the same God, beloved. The. Same. God.

He invites us to bring our questions to Him, the King of kings, assuring us, "Ask and it will be given to you; seek and you will find."[22]

When I asked our sisters on social media, "What question would you ask God?" their responses were profound, heartfelt, and often weighted with sorrow.

Some were universal in nature, the sort of questions we all might ask. Lori wonders, "Why is there cancer?" And Jena asks with a plaintive note in her words, "Why don't You end child abuse?"

Some questions reveal a sense of wonder or longing. Janet wants to understand, "Why did You create us?" Dori is eager to find out, "How can I help others know You as I do?" Megan asks wistfully, "How much longer until You come back, Lord?"

Many of the questions were more personal—and even more poignant. Julee's question is whispered like a prayer: "Why am I alone?" Michelle wonders, "What is the purpose of my husband's joblessness?" Becky's heartache shows when she asks, "Why do people lay in a nursing home for years without any knowledge of what's going on around them?" Dawn's request tears at our hearts: "May I please have a relationship with my granddaughter?" And Darlene's too: "Why did You let my son die when You could have saved him?"

I have a question or two of my own. "How can You be everywhere at once, Lord, yet meet each of our individual needs?" And from a deeper place,

"If my father rejected You to the very end of his life, how can I bear the thought of where he is now?"

In His perfect timing God can and will answer each of our questions. Faith in Him keeps our hope alive. Trust in Him helps us wait. If a mortal king like Solomon had an endless supply of answers, imagine what our divine God has in store for us!

SOLOMON THE WISE

When we're looking for a wise person, we aren't talking about a wise guy, someone who's crafty and shrewd, insolent and rude. We mean a person who has deep understanding, keen discernment, and the ability to make sound judgments.

Sheba no doubt had a bevy of wise men in her homeland. But she went to the top of the wisdom chain. She went to King Solomon, armed with her hardest questions.

If Sheba thought the man might cave in defeat, then surprise, surprise.

. . . nothing was too hard for the king . . . 1 Kings 10:3

"No matter how difficult it was" (CEV), Solomon sorted it out. No subject was "too obscure" (EXB); no riddle was "too complex" (NET). Whatever she threw at him and however elevated her vocabulary, "there was not any word the king was ignorant of" (DRA). The Hebrew word translated "too hard" actually means "to conceal," which makes this the most literal translation: "there was nothing hidden from the king" (AMP).

He unveiled mysteries. He revealed truth. When Sheba opened her heart, the anointed writer who likely penned Ecclesiastes, the Song of Songs, and most of Proverbs opened his mind and his mouth.

. . . to explain to her. 1 Kings 10:3

Here's the mark of a good counselor. Solomon didn't simply answer her. He made it "plain to her" (NLV). He went out of his way to "share with her" (WYC) all the whys and hows of things. In this scene the Bible doesn't sketch a portrait of a prideful man trying to impress. Instead, Solomon seemed intent on showing his royal visitor the depths of God's wisdom, leaving no avenue unexplored, no question unanswered.

Did Sheba give up? Climb on her camel and ride home? She did not. Our Sheba was bold, she was open, and she'd come with fragrant spices to seek wise counsel. So far, mission accomplished. Now that Solomon had "won the battle of wits,"[23] Sheba was pleased to learn all he knew. "Perfume and incense bring joy to the heart, and the pleasantness of a friend springs from their heartfelt advice."[24]

KNOW IT ALL

Think of the most brilliant person you know. The most intelligent, the most educated, the most well read. You could still bring up a topic that would stump him or her, right? When I mentioned to a renowned New Testament scholar that I was writing a book about the queen of Sheba, he responded, "Is she in the Bible?"

My first (and unkind) thought was *Good grief. You have a PhD!*

The Lord quickly got my attention. *This servant of Mine knows Matthew to Revelation intimately. He doesn't need to know about the queen of Sheba. You do.*

A humbling reminder. In the body of Christ, no one knows everything. As Queen Elizabeth II put it, "None of us has a monopoly of wisdom."[25] Even if we read God's Word beginning to end year after year, we will never master the whole of it.

Yet here is Solomon, able to provide all the answers because what he shared with Sheba wasn't his own wisdom. It was the Lord's. A gift from God to glorify Himself and to draw Sheba into His presence so "she might be persuaded to serve the Lord whom she now sought."[26]

Sheba was a true seeker, looking for God even if she wasn't fully aware of it. "The impulse that drives her is not unlike the one that drives our own quest."[27] In a sense we're all seekers longing for answers.

He Goes Before Us

Sometimes God sends counselors our way before we realize we need them.

Years ago when I was as lost in the world's darkness as any soul could be, two people stepped into my life. A husband and wife, new to the faith, were eager to share God's grace with anyone who stood still long enough. They snagged my wandering heart and held me in place with their sincere attention and genuine affection. They cared about me as a person rather than treating me as if I were a trophy to be won.

Because of that, I listened to them. I trusted them. Finally I believed them.

They remained in my life for a handful of months, then moved to another city two thousand miles away. This was a decade before the Internet, two decades before smart phones, so staying in touch meant expensive long-distance phone calls or plane tickets I couldn't afford.

At the time, I was undone. No more spiritual parents? No more wise counselors?

As the months passed, a light dawned. God wanted me to go directly to Him for wise counsel, to depend on Him for answers, to turn to His Word for direction. As Shelly wisely said online, "True healing comes when we learn to take our needs to our Mighty Counselor!"

Earthly teachers still play an important role, instructing us with their lives as much as their words. They lead us through the Scriptures, leaving enough breathing space so the Holy Spirit can confirm what is being taught and add a more personal application. When I'm taking notes, I may jot down what the teacher says, but I definitely write out everything the Holy Spirit impresses upon me.

If God is calling us to make major changes in our lives, then it's time to seek a wise, trustworthy believer to help us pray and prepare before we take the next step. Offering wise counsel doesn't mean always saying nice things, easy things. Sometimes it means saying hard things.

Not long after I embraced Christ as my Savior, I began dating a man who I knew deep down was not the Lord's choice for me. But I was single. He was handsome. I was thirty. He was available. How could this be a bad thing?

I met with a close friend to pray, fearful of what she might say. She said it anyway. "This relationship needs to end, Liz."

It wasn't what I wanted to hear. But it was what I needed to hear.

She told me the truth because she cared about me and because she loved the Lord, who urges us to "spur one another on toward love and good deeds."[28] We prayed, we wept, and then I followed her godly advice.

Make no mistake, it was painful. Especially when he married someone else a few months later (ouch). Then I met Bill, the man of my prayers. Am I grateful for that friend's wise counsel? Every day of my life.

WISE WOMEN SEEK WISE COUNSELORS

The challenge for most of us is, how do we find someone with the wisdom of Solomon to answer our questions and give us direction? Whether we need a career advisor, a life coach, a spiritual mentor, a Bible-study teacher, a Christian counselor, a brainstorming partner, or simply someone to be a sounding board, it's hard to know where to start or whom to trust.

Sherry offered her guidelines: "I look for someone who is grounded in his or her faith in God, who has experience with the issue or situation I'm dealing with, and who is trustworthy, encouraging, loving, and caring." Good checklist.

Now it's your turn. Anytime you have a problem that needs a solution or you long for solid advice or godly input, who is the first person you reach out to?

When I asked this question online, hundreds of women were quick to share where they seek wise counsel. More than half of us turn to a close friend. For those of us who are married, our husbands are next on the list, then a mother, pastor, sister, counselor.

Many of us prefer someone older, a been-there-done-that woman. Lidia expressed "a huge need for a godly, older-than-me woman who could be my spiritual mentor." Chris agrees: "I wish more older women in the church were willing to mentor younger women who still have kids at home and need advice."

Katy tugged at my heart when she admitted, "I have no one."

If you, like Katy, feel you have nowhere to turn, please know that you have a "Wonderful Counselor,"[29] who longs for you to "call on him while he is near."[30]

In seeking Him you'll find the One you're looking for.

Sheba did, though not before He brought her to her knees.

*D*o not let the costly silk threads in my robes or the sparkling jewels in my crown fool you. I am a woman undone. And I have no one to blame but myself.

My advisors warned me before we departed. *King Solomon is wealthy beyond counting, Your Majesty. Wise past imagining.* Alas, I did not believe them, not fully. I assumed they were exaggerating in an effort to unsettle me, perhaps even to discourage me from seeking his counsel.

Now I sit at Solomon's table, laden with golden platters of exotic foods and wine made from the sweetest grapes on earth, and I cannot think of a single word to say, let alone something witty or wise.

Why did no one tell me Solomon's glory exceeded my own?

We did, Queen. But you did not listen.

I glance down at my hands, tightly clasped in my lap. Pride. That's what Father would have said and what Mother always cautioned me against. "Hold up your head, Daughter, but do not think there is no one greater than you."

Solomon leans across the table now, interrupting my thoughts, offering a honeyed pear from his own hands. Day after day he has been a gracious host, pouring out his store of wisdom as easily as his cupbearers pour cup after generous cup.

The first time we conversed, Solomon began with a most perplexing riddle: "The fear of the LORD is the beginning of knowledge."[1] How can that be? I duly fear our many gods, but that does not lead to knowledge. It leads to more fear.

Solomon also told me that the fear of God is "a fountain of life"[2] rather than a harbinger of death. It is a puzzle beyond human understanding.

As I bring the sweet pear to my lips, Solomon watches me closely, not bothering to hide a smile. He sees my confusion. He knows what I am only now discovering:

I cannot decipher the wise sayings of Solomon until I fear the God he serves.

Sheba

Four

It's
Good
to Be
Humbled

When the queen of Sheba saw all the
wisdom of Solomon and the palace he had
built, the food on his table, the seating of
his officials, the attending servants in their
robes, his cupbearers, and the burnt offerings he made at the temple of the LORD, she
was overwhelmed.

1 KINGS 10:4–5

When I stepped through the door of my friend's new home, I felt exactly as Sheba did: overwhelmed. Every room was perfection, every piece of furniture exquisite. The deck, the pool, the view—all left me awestruck. But her walk-in closet did me in. It was the size of our living room, with sleek drawers and recessed lighting and dozens upon dozens of wooden hangers on slender silver bars lining *all four walls.*

Oh. My. Goodness.

I wasn't jealous or envious. Honest. I was just humbled at the thought of our old farmhouse, with its tiny closets full of cubbyholes and rusty hooks, its sloping floors and crooked doors. The home I loved suddenly seemed frumpy in comparison. Less than. Inadequate.

It is one thing to be *humble,* to willingly bow our heads and hearts, just as the Word tells us: "Humble yourselves, therefore, under God's mighty hand."[3] But it's something else again to be *humbled.* To get knocked down a peg.

That's what happened to Sheba.

She arrived in Jerusalem with her impressive entourage in tow, with her look polished to a high sheen, with her costly spices scenting the air—only to discover that Solomon laid claim to far more than she'd envisioned. More wisdom, more wealth, more servants, and an infinitely more powerful God.

Why is it good to be humbled? From that lower posture we're forced to look up—beyond this world and all its trappings—and see "the One who sits enthroned on high."[4] When we're on our knees, pressed there by God's loving hand, we finally grasp the superior Intelligence we are dealing with: the One who says, "As the heavens are higher than the earth, so are My ways higher than your ways and My thoughts than your thoughts."[5]

BRAIN TRUST

Solomon's buildings and furnishings were splendid, but what really stole Sheba's breath was the exceptional mind that "envisioned and constructed" (Voice) so fine a design.

> When the queen of Sheba saw all the wisdom
> of Solomon . . . *1 Kings 10:4*

Nothing has greater impact than seeing something with our own eyes. Sheba "perceived" (EXB) and "experienced for herself" (MSG) the man's "extensive wisdom" (NET). Before her long journey north, she'd had only the reports from her traders and her fertile imagination to go on. Now Sheba had "incontestable proofs"[6] of Solomon's vast knowledge and keen discernment.

I'm an educated woman, grateful for whatever gray matter the Lord has given me. But when I'm in the company of really brainy people, I shut down. Even as I smile and nod, inside I'm shrinking. *Please, Lord, help me not say the wrong thing and make a fool of myself.*

If you've been down that road in some social setting, then you know how Sheba must have felt. Intimidated. Perhaps a bit embarrassed. And definitely humbled. Who was this God who bestowed such powers of intellect and observation on Israel's king?

HOUSE PARTY

As if his wisdom weren't enough, Solomon's lodgings were also over-the-top amazing.

> . . . and the palace he had built, . . . *1 Kings 10:4*

It was a "house" (ASV), all right, and a good deal more, since the man "maintained an expensive lifestyle."[7] In fact, his "beautiful palace" (ERV) was the equal of royal residences found in Egypt, Persia, and Mesopotamia.[8]

The centerpiece was the throne room. In front of it stood a broad porch of pillars, where people milled about, waiting for an audience with the king. Inside, Solomon's magnificent throne was probably made of wood, overlaid with carved ivory panels, and then overlaid with gold, since "silver was considered of little value in Solomon's days."[9]

Seated six steps above the floor, Solomon could look down at his people while resting his sandals on a footstool of gold. Two carved lions flanked the arms of his throne, with more images of lions on each side, reminding all who entered of Solomon's strength.[10]

Clever man that he was, he placed his living quarters within a courtyard directly behind the throne room, allowing for a blessedly short commute at the end of his workday.

And what of his nightly banquets? Yes, please. We must talk more about those.

HAUTE CUISINE

> . . . the food on his table, . . . *1 Kings 10:5*

In particular, "the meats of his table" (WYC) were served only in the wealthiest households. Solomon's guests would have dined on fatted calf and lamb, goat and mutton, pigeon and dove, partridge and quail, gazelle and antelope.[11] These savory meat delicacies weren't offered only on the first night of Sheba's visit but were part of the daily provision for the king's table,[12] prepared according to sophisticated recipes preserved on ancient clay tablets.[13]

Beyond the cuisine, Sheba was amazed by "the variety and the elegance of the table settings,"[14] gleaming from one end of the banquet hall to the other, since "all King Solomon's goblets were gold."[15] Can you fathom such a sight? Little wonder Sheba was dazzled.

WHO'S WHO IN JERUSALEM

Our queen was no doubt seated at Solomon's right hand, a spot reserved for the most honored guest.[16] And she was surrounded by a multitude, because dining at the king's table was an opportunity extended to many of Jerusalem's elite.

> . . . the seating of his officials, . . . *1 Kings 10:5*

We sense her looking up and down the long table, counting those present and marveling at the number—a measurable sign of Solomon's influence.[17] His chief officials included Ahishar, his palace administrator; Benaiah, his commander in chief; and Adoniram, who was in charge of forced labor.[18]

There was also an orderliness to the "seating of his courtiers,"[19] each one in his appointed place. Rather like walking into a banquet and finding the tables carefully arranged with a name card for each guest. It avoids that awkward dance of deciding which table to join, where to land. At Solomon's palace the seating was well sorted before anyone arrived.

Whether they were "court officials" (MSG) or "servants" (NASB) or "slaves" (JUB), they were his subjects. The wealthier among them would have been handsomely dressed in fringed robes, wearing armlets and bracelets,[20] the polished metals and precious jewels catching the light of the oil lamps.

On a recent trip to the Holy Land, my tour group was invited to celebrate *Shabbat*—the Sabbath—with a Friday evening meal in a Jewish home. The table was covered with delicious foods and surrounded by lively company, but what I remember most was our hosts' bright-eyed young daughter standing at the top of the stairs as we entered, announcing, "More people! More people! More people!"

We could definitely use her talents now as we prepare the way for . . . well, more people.

OH, WAITER!

> . . . the attending servants in their
> robes, . . . *1 Kings 10:5*

Picture Solomon's "palace staff" (GNT) standing a polite distance behind his dinner guests,[21] ready to serve at the flick of a hand or the slightest nod. Not quite *Downton Abbey* but close.

The proper "manner" (CJB) in which these men served was commendable, but "the good clothes they wore" (ERV) were even more noteworthy. Think of them as "sharply dressed waiters" (MSG) wearing "uniforms" (GNT) that set them apart for the king's service.

Uniforms? In the tenth century BC? Yes, indeed. "The multitude of Solomon's retainers and the sumptuousness of their official liveries provided the queen of Sheba and others with graphic proof of his wealth and power."[22] This wasn't about Solomon's fashion sense. He wanted to impress both close allies and distant enemies. If you and I are talking about his waiters' apparel three thousand years later, word clearly got around the ancient Near East during Solomon's heyday.

WINE, WOMAN, AND SONG

No evening meal was complete without the best wine being brought to the table.

> . . . his cupbearers, . . . *1 Kings 10:5*

These "personal servants" (CJB) had a very specific assignment. They tasted and then poured Solomon's finest wine into "magnificent drinking-cups . . . filled from a great wine-bowl at one end of the chamber."[23] As Sheba watched "how the wine went round" (Knox), these servants handled their task with exceptional decorum and propriety.[24] Not a drop fell on her jewel-trimmed garments.

If you're concerned how the Lord fits into all this drinking and feasting, His Word assures us that Solomon's religious faith was on even greater display: "Three times a year Solomon sacrificed burnt offerings and fellowship offerings on the altar he had built for the LORD."[25]

More than once my family has complained about the burnt offerings I've served at mealtime, but in Solomon's case sacrifices were an important element of worship. And the queen of Sheba was there to watch it all unfold.

ON THE ALTAR

> . . . and the burnt offerings he made at the temple
> of the LORD, . . . *1 Kings 10:5*

Called *olah* in Hebrew—"whole burnt offerings" (EXB)—each sheep or goat placed on the altar was a male without blemish.[26] The rising smoke of the offering, which was entirely consumed by the flames, represented "the ascent of the soul in worship,"[27] which is why so many translations speak of Solomon's "ascent" (AMP) or "entryway" (NKJV) into a true state of worship.

But Sheba didn't see goats and lambs and smoke and ash. She saw Israel's king with "an air of devotion in his countenance"[28] and observed him worshiping the Lord with holy reverence and heartfelt gladness.

Whatever incense Sheba burned to her many gods, her piety was no match for Solomon's. Otherwise, his love for God wouldn't have left her gasping for air.

BREATHLESS

. . . she was overwhelmed. 1 Kings 10:5

Our wealthy, powerful queen was left stunned and speechless, "breathless and overcome" (AMP), by the religious fervor of her host. "She could hardly believe everything she had seen" (NIrV)—his sacrifices, his solemn prayers, his bowed head, his humble heart.

Solomon was king, yet he honored One higher! Unheard of in that time and place when many sovereigns thought themselves gods.

Sheba stood there, "amazed" (NCV) by all she'd seen and "in complete awe" (Voice) of the earthly and heavenly blessings heaped on Solomon's head by this unseen God. Perhaps her eyes were wide "in wonder" (Knox) or her mouth hung slack with astonishment, for no *ruach,* or "breath" (OJB), remained. Indeed, "there was no more spirit in her" (ASV).

The queen of Sheba hadn't died. Or had she?

Is it possible that the spirits of Sheba's old gods departed at that moment, making way for the Spirit of the Lord to take residence in her heart? Scholars tell us she experienced an "extremely strong emotion"[29] as the frequency and sincerity of "the temple ceremonies overwhelmed her."[30]

In all her travels Sheba had never seen "so much goodness with so much greatness."[31] Solomon wasn't merely a man of wisdom; he was also a man of remarkable faith, whose "words are matched by his deeds."[32]

Sheba was fresh out of questions, her pride utterly dismantled, and for a very good purpose—God's purpose.

HUMBLED BY HIM

The Lord showed us the way when He "humbled himself by becoming obedient to death—even death on a cross!"[33] Who better to teach us the cost of humility?

Jesus said, "Those who exalt themselves will be humbled, and those who humble themselves will be exalted."[34] For all his wisdom and wealth, Solomon still humbled himself, walked in obedience, and worshiped the Lord. Sheba arrived with her wits and her gold on display, only to be humbled by a God who was slowly but surely drawing her into His embrace.

He draws us too, beloved, and He holds us close.

Online, Julie shared her experience as a caregiver for her elderly mother, which turned out to be "a crash course in humility. To lay down your life for another is a tall order, but I'm finding it is refining and growing me in ways I never imagined."

The truth? Only the deeply spiritual among us are excited about being humbled. The rest of us slowly let go of our pride, knowing we need to be humbled even if we haven't eagerly signed up for it.

FLOOR LEVEL

One November I traveled to the Dominican Republic, invited by a missionary friend to speak at a gathering of sisters and seekers who were ready to hear more about Jesus. I was *so in*.

An hour after I landed in the Dominican Republic, I'd fallen in love with her people. They were warm, gracious, kind. Their houses were painted like flowers. Their hearts were wide open.

A small group of women from the United States had flown down for the weekend to help with the conference. We filled the church van on Friday morning and headed for town, eager to see the ministry's new sanctuary.

I pictured a freshly painted building, still smelling faintly of sawdust. What we pulled up to was an old brewery, still smelling faintly of . . . well . . . lots of things, thanks to the overflowing garbage cans in the alley.

When they opened the door, I did my best to hide my dismay. The place looked more industrial than spiritual. And the concrete floor was (sorry) filthy. Still, the space had character. Fabulous windows with huge, rustic shutters. A low platform with a vintage rug and piano. But something had to be done about that floor before we filled the place with women in their Sunday-best shoes.

"Let's tackle the floor first!" one volunteer said brightly. I smiled, thinking what a grand idea that was. Then they handed everyone a broom. Including me.

Here comes the ugly, embarrassing, I-hate-to-tell-you-this part of the story. I have been invited to speak at hundreds of churches, but I'd never before been asked to clean one. So while I was smiling on the outside (or at least trying), on the inside I was thinking *Seriously? You want me to wash the floor?*

I could hardly do otherwise with my American sisters joyfully diving in. One woman threw soapy water across the concrete, and we came behind her with our budget brooms, pushing the dirty water toward the door.

Everybody else was having a blast, singing praise songs as they worked. Me? I was one sweaty, drippy, unhappy mess. By the time I reached the area directly in front of the platform, I'd had it right up to my mud-splattered knees.

"Lord," I grumbled under my breath, "I'm the guest speaker. Can't they get someone else to do this?"

His response pierced my heart. *Liz, I thought you wanted to serve Me.*

My eyes filled with tears. *I do, Lord. I do want to serve You.* Wasn't that why I'd come to the Dominican Republic? To serve Him by loving His daughters? What was I thinking, putting myself above His other servants?

Jesus told his followers, "Unless I wash you, you have no part with me."[35] I needed washing more than the floor did.

God humbles us so we will know our place and willingly receive His gift of grace. Then we can "draw near to God with a sincere heart and with the full assurance that faith brings, having our hearts sprinkled to cleanse us from a guilty conscience and having our bodies washed with pure water."[36] Doesn't it feel wonderful to be clean?

Only after Sheba was humbled do her spoken words appear in Scripture. It's as if she finally had something to say—something worth remembering, worth recording for the ages. Now that she'd caught a glimpse of God through His servant Solomon, she was ready to put aside queenly posturing and speak from her heart.

*S*olomon is looking at me now, eyebrows arched. Waiting.

I adjust the layers of silk pooling at my feet, as if I might find the words I need inside the colorful folds. Where shall I begin? How can I explain?

"I beg your pardon, Solomon . . ." "I was misinformed . . ." "I was unprepared . . ."

No. This very morning the king taught me, "An honest witness tells the truth."[1] After all the marvels I have seen and heard in Jerusalem, I cannot feign disinterest or blame another for my foolishness.

Still, to confess my prideful assumptions about his kingdom here, among his people. What will they think of the Queen of the South then?

All at once something shifts inside me, then gently falls into place. *It only matters what the king thinks.* A sense of rightness settles in. A certainty I have not felt before.

Solomon has told me, "Blessed are those who find wisdom, those who gain understanding,"[2] and that is precisely how I feel at this moment. Humbled, yet also blessed by Solomon, perhaps even by his God. Is such a thing possible?

My head lifts. Any lingering sense of pride or pretense is swept away like sand on a hot desert wind. I know what must be said and am surprised to find I am ready to say it.

Solomon is nodding at me. It is time.

Sheba

Five

It's
Good
to Be
Honest

❦

She said to the king, "The report I heard
in my own country about your achievements and your wisdom is true. But I did
not believe these things until I came and
saw with my own eyes. Indeed, not even
half was told me; in wisdom and wealth
you have far exceeded the report I heard."

1 Kings 10:6–7

Nothing reveals our true character like the words that pour out of our mouths, because they come from the depths of our souls: "For the mouth speaks what the heart is full of."³ Full of ugly? Out comes ugly. Full of truth? Out comes truth.

Sheba's first recorded words are an honest confession, spoken directly to King Solomon. She could have kept her niggling doubts about his great wealth and wisdom to herself. Or written them in her personal chronicles. Or shared them in a letter to a trustworthy confidant in her home country.

But Sheba was a truth teller. She went straight to Solomon and fessed up.

She said to the king, . . . *1 Kings 10:6*

Remember how breathless Sheba was a moment earlier? The words she was about to speak must have burst from her lips. She didn't just talk—she "exclaimed" (NLT).

The king's face surely lit up at Sheba's forthrightness. Perhaps she was the person Solomon had in mind when he wrote, "Kings take pleasure in honest lips; they value the one who speaks what is right."⁴ The proverb certainly suits her. However much Solomon appreciated the costly gifts Sheba would lay at his feet, her honesty and wisdom pleased him more. "Gold there is, and rubies in abundance, but lips that speak knowledge are a rare jewel."[5]

That's our Sheba. A one-of-a-kind woman. A priceless gem.

Then she put her thoughts into words, preserved for eternity.

THIS JUST IN

"The report I heard in my own country . . ." 1 Kings 10:6

What Sheba had heard wasn't gossip; it was "news" (NLV). So remarkable were the "stories" (ERV) that had reached the queen while she was "still at home" (CEB), they compelled her to travel north. Sadly, when today's news goes viral, it's often shocking or tragic or memorable for all the wrong reasons. But the reports about Solomon were both positive and accurate, as Sheba discovered when she came to test him.

Now I am the one who's humbled. How often have I caught wind of some news about a person and taken it as truth without investigating it? If I heard it from a friend, if I read it online, if I saw it in the paper, it must be legit. Right?

Sheba's determination to stick with the truth challenges us to dig deeper and speak only from experience, especially if a person's character is being discussed. It's not enough to *hear.* We need to *see.* We need to *know.*

Because she'd watched those stories about Solomon become reality before her eyes, Sheba could affirm all she'd been told.

". . . about your achievements and your
wisdom is true." 1 Kings 10:6

Solomon's greatest accomplishments weren't his massive building projects, his twelve-thousand-man cavalry, his fourteen hundred chariots.[6] Rather they were his words, his "wise sayings and insight" (NET), which were "beyond extraordinary" (Voice).

Sheba crowed with obvious delight, "It's all true!" (MSG). The news she'd received was now "confirmed" (MSG)—from the Hebrew word *emeth*, meaning "firmness, faithfulness."

Then she made a heartfelt admission.

UH-OH

"But I did not believe these things . . ."

1 Kings 10:7

Did Sheba take a deep breath before she said this? She was certainly courageous when she "freely confessed"[7] her initial response to the glowing reports about Solomon: "I gave no credence to the words" (YLT).

Of all the rulers who heard about Solomon's wisdom, Sheba is the only one on record as having questioned what she heard.[8] She needed to be convinced that Solomon was wise, that his God was real. She'd traveled to Jerusalem to test him, bringing with her a certain skepticism, a reluctance to embrace what she hadn't personally seen or experienced.[9]

The Hebrew word translated "believe" also means "to confirm, support." Sheba did none of those things at the start and boldly told him so. "When I first heard of your renown, I did not believe such a man could really be alive on the earth" (Voice).

Wow, girl. Sure you want to say that to this powerful king?

There are other ways she might have worded this and not risked Solomon's disapproval. But Sheba shelved her pride, ditched her embarrassment, and spoke the truth, holding nothing back.

This is what we need to learn from her. This is what she teaches us by example.

HONESTY IS THE ONLY POLICY

Job proclaimed, "How painful are honest words!"[10] It's especially painful to say them aloud. "I was wrong." "I didn't believe." By God's design our mistakes are meant to humble us—and they usually succeed.

When I chatted with our sisters online about why it's tough to admit we've made a mistake, Lisa said, "I don't mind admitting when I'm wrong; I just hate *knowing* I was wrong." Our mistakes often haunt us, playing over and over in our minds. God forgives and forgets, yet we can't manage to do either.

Here's a promise we need to cling to: "For as high as the heavens are above the earth, so great is his love for those who fear him; as far as the east is from the west, so far has he removed our transgressions from us."[11] His love reaches high enough. His grace stretches far enough. He not only sets the bar. He also leaps over it for us.

Still, we struggle.

Karla confessed, "It all comes down to pride. When admitting I'm wrong, I'm also admitting I'm not as great a person as I want others to think I am." Right there with you, sister. Oh, the lengths we will go to make ourselves look good. It takes a woman of courage to show the world her flaws and failures.

Hollie admits, "All my insecurities come to the surface: feeling inadequate, unintelligent, thoughtless." And Susan says, "I dread appearing vulnerable—like maybe I don't know everything." For sure, I would much rather look as if I have it all together and never make mistakes. But as the Bible cautions us, "If we claim to be without sin, we deceive ourselves and the truth is not in us."[12]

Since honesty is what we're after, self-deception has to go.

As Brenda sees it, "Some people will never admit they are wrong—to themselves or others. Some people get defensive and make excuses for their mistakes, trying to make themselves feel better. And some people are truly afraid to be wrong."

SCARED TO BE HONEST

I believe pride is at the root of all our sin. Buried beneath that pride is often deep-seated fear. What are we afraid will happen if we admit we're wrong? Cynthia "struggles with the unknown. What will others think of me? What will their reactions be? Will they still look at me in a positive light?"

Here's the list of fears our sisters carry in their hearts—fears that keep us from saying, "I made a mistake."

Abandonment	Judgment
Criticism	Lack of empathy
Embarrassment	Loss of respect
Gloating	Rejection
Gossip	Ridicule
Humiliation	Unwanted advice

Some fears can't be reduced to a word or two. Chris said she's worried people might "hesitate to ask my opinion in the future." Jane dreads "living with someone else's resentment and anger" and "having that person punish me with cold silence." Beth fears "the relationship with that other person will never be the same."

These fears are real. Many are well founded. When we fail in a big way, people might not trust our judgment or might treat us differently for a season. But in time honesty and humility will soften their hearts. They will learn from our example and, if they are brave, will follow in our footsteps when the time comes.

For Carla the toughest part is "realizing that my goal of perfection just keeps getting further and further away." Maybe that's a good thing. The sooner we embrace this truth, the better. On our own we will never reach perfection, but in Christ we are made perfect—that is, we are *complete*. God's Word tells us, "He is the Rock, his works are perfect."[13]

God is still shaping us into the image of His Son, a process that continues until the moment we step into His heavenly presence. But our salvation is a completed work. In fact, "his works have been finished since the creation of the world."[14]

We see only our faults. God sees only His forgiveness, poured out like one of Sheba's fragrant oils—refreshing, soothing, cleansing, healing.

FROM FEAR TO FREEDOM

Ask women who have owned up to their mistakes, and they'll tell you, as Michelle does, "Confessing your faults and errors can be very liberating. It also helps you grow a stronger, more honest character." That's what we're aiming for, yes? Honesty and strength, the kind only God can provide. "For the eyes of the LORD range throughout the earth to strengthen those whose hearts are fully committed to him."[15]

Beverly writes, "I love the freedom that comes from admitting that I'm wrong, that I'm the one who did it. I can take the blame and learn from my mistakes." And Mary promises, "When it is done, it is total relief."

Sometimes we don't seek that relief right away. Days, weeks, months, even years may go by. We fear we've waited too long to make it right.

Good news: it's never too late.

Many years ago a young elementary teacher sent home a note with my daughter, chastising me for traveling too much and insisting, "She misses you when you're gone." The fact that my husband worked from home and was a very involved father didn't seem to matter. I was single-handedly ruining my daughter's childhood.

The teacher's words cut deep, prompting me to question my calling, my ministry, my mothering, my whole way of doing life. I had already trimmed back my speaking calendar. *Should I do even fewer events, Lord? Should I stop speaking altogether?*

After much prayer I arrived at a place of peace, even as our sweet girl continued to blossom. Still, the words in that note never completely left my mind.

Twelve years later when our daughter was graduating from high school, I got an unexpected phone call: her elementary teacher, reaching out to apologize. "I wasn't a mother then," she said in a soft voice, "and I didn't understand. Now I do. I just wanted to say . . . I'm sorry."

Astounded that she'd even remembered that note, I forgave her at once. Then I told her how grateful I was for her courage and how impressed I was with her tender heart. I'm not sure my words made a great deal of sense, what with the tissues and all. Her honesty touched me deeply, and her humility more so.

We'd both carried the guilt of that note long enough.

Her willingness to speak the truth set us both free.

If we fearlessly live out our faith, even our failures give us an opportunity to glorify God. As He assured the apostle Paul, so He assures us: "My grace is sufficient for you, for my power is made perfect in weakness."[16]

Amy says, "Being wrong solidifies my desperate need for a Savior! I can admit I'm wrong and not be destroyed by it." And Lynn has discovered, "When I confess, God makes all things right, including my heart."

Listen as Sheba's admission continues, and hear the note of freedom ringing through her words.

EYE OPENING

". . . until I came and saw with my own eyes." *1 Kings 10:7*

She offered no regret about her long journey, despite the sacrifice of time and expense. "I came myself" (DRA), she declared firmly, and "my eyes have seen" (JUB). When Sheba beheld the glory of Solomon, perhaps she glimpsed in his countenance the glory of the Lord.

At the dedication of the temple sometime before her arrival, "Solomon finished praying, . . . and the glory of the LORD filled the temple."[17] Oh, the splendor! God's glory, wrapped "in a dark cloud,"[18] fell on His temple in Jerusalem.

We can hear the awe in Solomon's words: "But will God really dwell on earth? The heavens, even the highest heaven, cannot contain you. How much less this temple I have built!"[19] Even so, God filled Solomon's temple, just as He fills His people with the Holy Spirit. "Don't you know that you yourselves are God's temple and that God's Spirit dwells in your midst?"[20]

Sheba was starting to get the big picture: *everything* about Solomon was about God. "I wouldn't have believed it if I hadn't seen it for myself,"[21] she told him, glad she'd come and grateful for what she'd found. "I have witnessed your greatness with my own eyes, and I believe" (Voice).

Did she believe at that moment in the one true God of Israel? We'll wait for more proof, but one thing is certain: Solomon, like his father before him, was loved by God and radiant with His blessings. Sheba was drawn to that light. Warmed by it. Dazzled by it. She longed to grasp "what no eye has seen, what no ear has heard, and what no human mind has conceived."[22]

HEAR, SEE, BELIEVE

Then Sheba made another confession. She wasn't pinning blame on herself or anyone else, but the full account of Solomon's greatness hadn't made it to her homeland.

"Indeed, not even half was told me; . . ." *1 Kings 10:7*

Maybe some of the news was lost in transit or seemed so unbelievable no one dared tell the whole of it to their queen. "It's amazing!" (ISV) she said, exuberant. "There's so much I didn't hear about" (CEV). Sheba realized "half of it was lost in the telling" (Knox), and once she'd seen the truth firsthand, she told Solomon, "Now I believe it!" (NIrV).

We're reminded of the Samaritan woman who brought news of the Messiah back to her town following a life-changing encounter with Jesus at a well. After Jesus spent two days in their midst, the townspeople told her, "We no longer believe just because of what you said; now we have heard for ourselves, and we know that this man really is the Savior of the world."[23]

This is one of the patterns we find in Scripture: we hear with our ears, we see with our eyes, and then we are changed.

Job told the Lord, "My ears had heard of you but now my eyes have seen you."[24] And Jesus said to His disciples, "Blessed are your eyes because they see, and your ears because they hear."[25] In the same way, Sheba heard about wise Solomon and his relationship with God. Then she saw the glory of Solomon and his God, and she was changed.

As commentator Matthew Henry eloquently described this scene, "Those who, through grace, are brought to experience the delights of communion with God will say that the one-half was not told them of the pleasures of Wisdom's ways."[26]

OVER THE TOP

*". . . in wisdom and wealth you have far exceeded
the report I heard." 1 Kings 10:7*

Either she had heard only half the story, or Solomon was "twice as wise and wealthy" (NIrV) as the reports that had reached Ma'rib. "Such wisdom and elegance—far more than I could ever have imagined" (MSG), she admitted. "Here is greater wisdom, greater prosperity than all the tales that reached me" (Knox).

The queen of Sheba could have kept her astonishment to herself.

Pretended to be unimpressed. Shrugged as if to say "I've seen better." Bragged about her own wisdom, her own wealth. Reminded him of all the riches she would add to his coffers. Taken her leave without further discussion. Instead, she spoke with humility and honesty and "owned her expectation far out-done."[27]

God exceeds our expectations too. Time and again He does "immeasurably more than all we ask or imagine, according to his power that is at work within us."[28]

You'll remember how the Lord humbled me in the Dominican Republic as I swept water across the dirty floor of that church. Because of His loving-kindness, the Lord was willing to "wash away all my iniquity and cleanse me from my sin."[29] My pride, my stubbornness, my I'm-too-good-for-this attitude—all of it washed clean that Friday morning.

Overcome with gratitude for His mercy, I tackled the floor with renewed vigor, singing and laughing with the others as we turned an old brewery into a beautiful sanctuary.

The next morning three hundred women walked through the doors of the church, dressed in their best clothes. We spent all day together studying God's Word. It was joy unspeakable.

Near the end of the conference, I invited women to come forward for prayer. Slowly at first and then in greater numbers, they left their seats to meet with our prayer team.

But not the women in my front row. One by one they bowed their heads and knelt on the concrete floor. *Knelt.* Yes, there. Right in front of the platform, where God had met me in my sin and showered me with His grace.

Then He whispered to my heart. *See, Liz? You washed the floor for them.*

ON OUR KNEES

Ah, the sweetness of that moment. No matter how long we've known Him, the Lord continues to teach us, love us, humble us, restore us. In doing so, this God we serve never ceases to amaze us, surprise us, delight us, overwhelm us.

Sheba was honest with Solomon. Rather than trying to impress him, she confessed how fully he had impressed her. She willingly lowered herself to lift him higher. Can we learn from her example and do the same? Honor others and so honor God?

Paul urges us, "In humility value others above yourselves."[30] We're about to watch the queen of Sheba do exactly that.

*M*y dear girl, a queen must never weep in the company of others." Mother's words, spoken long ago and surely well meant. But she could not have guessed the depth of emotion I would plumb this day.

Having confessed the truth aloud to Solomon, my heart seems to have broken open—not in a painful way but a joyful one. Tears shimmer in my eyes, making everything around me appear brighter. In truth, the gilded walls are no match for the shining countenances of Solomon's people, as if they have seen something not of this world.

My subjects in Sheba are obedient, attentive, efficient. But they do not turn to me, faces aglow, waiting in breathless expectation for what I might say next. I am simply their queen, their sovereign, a woman who bears a scepter and wears a crown.

King Solomon is far more. He is servant to a heavenly King, the One he calls the true God. Do his people know how fortunate they are? They need not make sacrifices to multiple gods, hoping to appease them, but to one God, certain to please Him.

Their king is the wisest man alive. Truth falls from his lips like morning dew.

And I am thirsty for it. I am.

Even as I brush away tears, I smile at his subjects, thinking of what I might say to convince them that they are the most blessed people on earth.

Sheba

Six

It's
Good
to
Encourage
Others

How happy your people must be! How
happy your officials, who continually
stand before you and hear your wisdom!

1 KINGS 10:8

Sheba's humble confession quickly shifted into praise, blessing the king and everyone else within earshot. This verse in the original Hebrew had no punctuation, but it's clear why the translators added exclamation points. Read Sheba's words aloud, and you can hear the excitement in her voice and see her animated expression.

Eyes bright. Bejeweled hands sketching the air.

"How happy your people must be!" *1 Kings 10:8*

In a land where poetry and song were treasured, Sheba's words poured out like music: "O the happiness of thy men" (YLT) and "How blessed are your staff!" (ISV). Such a skilled diplomat, this woman. With a few words she complimented Solomon *and* all of Israel.

What leader doesn't want to be applauded for his or her abilities? And followers like to know their loyalty is well placed. "You backed the right guy!" Sheba told them. (That's the LRV, the Lizzie Revised Version.) Fully aware of the impact a wise ruler can have on his people, she called his subjects "blessed" (DRA), "very fortunate" (ERV), and "truly happy!" (CEB).

Sheba called it the way she saw it. Scripture tells the same story. Solomon's people "lived in safety, everyone under their own vine and under their own fig tree,"[1] where "they ate, they drank and they were happy."[2]

The king definitely made Sheba happy, listening to all that was on her heart, then answering her every question. She saw the truth with her own eyes—"a ruler with discernment and knowledge maintains order."[3] Because she marveled at the thought of being led by a wise king like Solomon, she praised his people for having that honor.

TRUE TO TYPE

Sheba's generous words and bold actions hint at her bigger-than-life persona. To better understand our queen, I turned to the Myers-Briggs Type Indicator, a well-established personality test.[4] With the help of a friend who is well versed in MBTI assessment, I determined Sheba was likely extroverted, intuitive, and skilled at thinking and judging—an ENTJ. That makes Sheba a rare bird, since less than 2 percent of people fall into that category, and most of them are men.[5]

Here are the qualities that make an ENTJ unique and the things we might surmise about the queen of Sheba:

Ready to lead—She was well suited to the throne and a gifted communicator.

Decisive—She made up her mind to test Solomon's wisdom and followed through.

Planner, goal setter—She orchestrated a fifteen-hundred-mile journey. With camels.

Well informed, well read—She knew all the right questions to ask.

Objective, logical—Her fine mind was on display more than her tender emotions.

Verbal—Her lengthy exchanges with Solomon and her spoken words prove it.

Frank—She was bold and honest with Solomon, unafraid to say what was on her mind.

Good judge of character—She observed and applauded the king and his subjects.

Confident—Certain of her own gifts and skills, she could celebrate another's talents and abilities.

No one is perfect, not even our honorable queen. A keen intellect can make a person arrogant or opinionated. Decisiveness can lead to rash decisions. And a gift with words might mean fewer listening skills. In the biblical story, we see no evidence of these weaknesses in Sheba, but rest assured, she had some. That doesn't make her less of a role model. It just makes her more like us. A real person, not a superhero.

JOB ONE

Sheba's good qualities weren't limited to her personality type, and neither are ours. In whatever ways we express ourselves, the Lord calls each of us to honor Him in what we say, think, and do.

Encouragement is a gift we're all called to share, living out God's command to "encourage one another daily."[6] Praising others is also a habit worth developing. As Solomon wrote, "Let someone else praise you, and not your own mouth; an outsider, and not your own lips."[7] And we're called to temper our words, ever considerate of others and looking for ways to edify them. "Words from the mouth of the wise are gracious."[8]

I saw all the above unfold one Sunday morning at church.

With Pastor Bill Hybels as our guest speaker, we anticipated a powerful sermon, which was duly delivered. But what I remember most is the first five minutes. He didn't toss off funny one-liners or talk about his family or tell us about his ministry.

He praised our pastor.

He assured us how blessed we were to have a man like Bob Russell in the pulpit every Sunday. He described the challenges of leadership and how ably Bob tackled them, the pitfalls of being in the public eye and how humbly Bob handled them.

Since Bob was preaching elsewhere that morning, Pastor Hybels's comments weren't aimed at the front row, meant to flatter. He simply spoke from the heart and helped us see our pastor as a person—and an exceptional one at that.

We all sat up straighter and beamed at one another. Hooray for Bob. Hooray for us.

That's precisely what Sheba did. She aimed her praise at the people who knew Solomon best.

SPREADING THE JOY

"How happy your officials, . . ." 1 Kings 10:8

Sheba continued dishing out kudos, this time singling out those closest to the king—his "servants" (ASV), his "attendants" (NET), even his many "wives" (EXB). We can picture Solomon acknowledging Sheba with a regal nod, perhaps even mouthing his thanks, as she bolstered his people's trust in their king.

Solomon keenly needed the support of these men and women who labored on his behalf since he'd executed his older half brother Adonijah in order to secure the throne.[9] How timely to have someone from outside the palace walls help his people see their work for him as a "privilege" (NLT) rather than a burden.

Sheba also understood the subtle difference between praise and encouragement. Praise says, "You did a good job!" It's the cherry on top of the ice-cream sundae. Encouragement says, "You can do a good job because ___!" It's the first scoop of ice cream, the foundation that supports everything else.

The queen of Sheba was the ideal candidate to encourage the king's people, reminding them of their blessed position. She spoke with authority and candor, knowing "Gracious words are a honeycomb, sweet to the soul and healing to the bones."[10]

The remarkable thing? We don't hear jealousy or envy in her words—only delight.

Envy is the opposite of encouragement. Envy looks for ways to tear down rather than build up, to diminish rather than increase. Some people are really good at discouragement. They dis people left and right in lame attempts to elevate themselves.

Encouragers focus on the positive. They seek goodness. They look to God. And they know their calling, their spiritual gifting. Although Paul's letter to the Romans was written a thousand years after Sheba's reign, she fully embraced these three spiritual gifts: "if it is to encourage, then give encouragement; if it is giving, then give generously; if it is to lead, do it diligently."[11] That's our sister, showing us how to do life right.

MOTIVE MATTERS

Not all encouragement is as genuine as Sheba's. Sometimes compliments come from people who want something from us. Their language smacks of insincerity—or worse, duplicity. Their words are suspect, their actions dubious, their approach manipulative. We brush off their false praise and wait for the request that's sure to follow.

But the wealthy and powerful Sheba had nothing to gain by praising Solomon. Her encouragement was offered without guile or pretense, free of any hidden agenda.

Can you always say the same, beloved? Can I?

See, I *love* to encourage people—friends and strangers alike—but Sheba's good intentions make me question my reasons for dishing out praise. Do I lift up others with no thought of how it might benefit me? Or am I secretly hoping they'll return the favor? Or (ugh) do I believe making *them* look good will somehow make *me* look good?

I hate the thought of it. Loathe the possibility of it staring me in the face.

Maybe you're worried about the same thing. Maybe it's time we asked God.

Show us, Lord. Is our encouragement toward others selfless? Or selfish? Are we focused on them? On You? On ourselves?

This we know: true encouragement flows from the heart of God, pure and clean like water from a mountain stream. "You, LORD, hear the desire of the afflicted; you encourage them, and you listen to their cry."[12] The Lord demonstrates how it's done, and then He calls, equips, and empowers us to do the same—to "encourage one another and build each other up."[13]

God intends encouragement to be a two-way street. Diane has found that "when we encourage someone else, we both feel better, we become closer, and we forge a bond of support." Luci believes encouragement "not only builds the other person up—it also helps build you up."

Let's think about *who* needs an uplifting word, *why* we feel called to step forward, and *how* we can make it all about them, not about us.

WHO NEEDS ENCOURAGEMENT?

Absolutely everybody needs to hear encouraging words. Not one person has waved me off, saying, "No thanks. I'm good." No way. We all need our hearts filled and our spirits lifted regularly.

Encouragement is optimism in action. It's Philippians 4:8 lived out: "Whatever is true, whatever is noble, whatever is right, whatever is pure, whatever is lovely, whatever is admirable—if anything is excellent or praiseworthy—think about such things."

One genuine word of encouragement can make a person's day, can build her confidence, can help him stay on track, can give her the courage to do something difficult, can raise his expectations of what happy surprises the day might hold.

Like the time a makeup artist informed me, "You have perfect lips."

"Perfect *what*?"

"Absolutely," she insisted, dabbing at my mouth with her lipstick brush. "With most people I have to pencil in those two little peaks. Yours came straight from heaven."

My perfect peaks were paralyzed with shock.

"Not only that," she continued, "but both sides are even, and the bottom lip is fuller than the top one. I'm telling you, they're perfect."

Talk about an encouraging word! When it comes to physical beauty, the most I'd ever hoped for was a good-looking pancreas or pleasantly opposing thumbs. But perfect lips?

Now whenever I'm feeling frumpy, I put on bright red lipstick, jump in front of a mirror, and smile big. "Ta-da!" Perfect.

Even an offhand comment can make a memorable difference.

WHY ENCOURAGE OTHERS?

The Bible compels us to "accept one another, then, just as Christ accepted you, in order to bring praise to God."[14] Elvie believes "the Lord allows and brings us through the troubles in our lives, not only to teach us about His faithfulness, but also so we can, in turn, share our experiences with others and encourage them."

The benefits to those we encourage are numberless. Diane says, "It affirms people's choices, helps them move forward, and shows them how God is working in their lives." Shirley calls encouragement "a selfless act of love that gives hope," and Alyssa has learned, "You can be God's voice to others who are finding it difficult to hear or recognize Him."

Amy's wise reminder? "It costs us nothing."

Making It All About the Lord

Telling someone "God has so gifted you!" gives Him the glory while still affirming the person's talent, skill, and dedication. By including His name in the conversation, we keep everyone's focus on Him. If others praise us instead of acknowledging God, it's up to us to gently point them in His direction.

This can backfire, of course.

Whenever I finish sharing a message from the platform, I quickly turn toward the back of the stage and lift my arms in praise to make sure the audience is clapping for God, not for me. (True confession: in my early years of speaking, I happily drank in all that applause until God showed me the error of my ways!)

The first time I spoke at a Women of Faith conference, I was determined to honor the Lord the moment that big arena full of women started clapping. At the end of my presentation, I raised my hands and whipped around, then realized to my horror that *my name* was on the screen behind me in *huge* letters. Mortified, I kept turning in circles until I spun into the wings and out of sight.

I'm pretty sure I heard God laughing.

He knew I meant well, right?

What Goes Around

If our hearts are in the right place, the benefits often come full circle. "When you take your focus off yourself and encourage someone else," Karen tells us, "the blessings you pour out splash back on you." You may discover, as Bette did, that "your own problems aren't so bad." And Jane Ann has found "God's presence is more real in my life when I forget myself and love others."

We can only guess what outcomes the queen of Sheba might have expected. She was busy affirming and blessing the people standing in front of her, always keeping her eye on Solomon, the prime recipient of her encouraging words.

IN THE PRESENCE OF THE KING

". . . who continually stand before you . . ." 1 Kings 10:8

Those in service to Solomon did a bunch of standing, a ton of serving, and lots of "attending" (CJB). They were stationed in front of their king and remained there "day after day" (NLT). Whether or not it was "forevermore" (WYC), it surely must have felt like it.

Had Solomon been evil like Ahab,[15] or cruel like Herod,[16] or foolish like Saul,[17] standing before him might have been a trial, if not an execution waiting to happen. But this king of Israel blessed those in his presence because of the wisdom that poured from his mouth.

Do you know someone like that? Maybe several someones? People you love to hang out with because the words they speak are intelligent or kind or thoughtful or uplifting or deeply spiritual or profoundly funny or challenging in the best way? If you have even one such friend, you are rich indeed.

Sheba was certain Solomon's court felt precisely that way about their sovereign.

". . . and hear your wisdom!" 1 Kings 10:8

Wisdom was Solomon's distinctive. By actual count "he spoke three thousand proverbs."[18] No wonder "the kings of the earth sought audience with Solomon to hear the wisdom God had put in his heart."[19] They knew where the wisdom came from. They knew it was not from Solomon but from One greater than he.

Just to "get to listen" (CEB) to the king was an honor, from where Sheba was standing. She'd been with him only a short time, but his people had been "privileged to hear" (GNT) his wise sayings "every day" (ERV)—not whispered up and down the streets of Jerusalem but from Solomon's own lips, "first-hand!" (MSG).

You and I have a far greater honor waiting for us every time we open God's Word. We hear from the Lord Himself. His words, His wisdom. Not secondhand, not second best. The very words of the Almighty.

You may be thinking, *Wait. What about the various translations of Scripture?*

The Holy Spirit has preserved the power of God's truth through every translation. How can we be sure of that? God never takes His hand off His Word. "Your word, LORD, is eternal; it stands firm in the heavens."[20] And by the power of His Holy Spirit, we "accepted it not as a human word, but as it actually is, the word of God, which is indeed at work in you who believe."[21]

When we encourage others, we live out the truth of His eternal Word in a real-world, hands-on way. Sheba honored Solomon with her words and with her gifts. And wait until you see where Sheba aimed her praise next!

I look at their faces bright with anticipation. They have always known what I have finally learned: the God of Israel is not only real; He is also sovereign. The one and only God. I can no longer deny it.

Dare I speak openly? Praise Him before His own people?

I eye my sleeve, wishing I could press the fabric to my damp cheeks. Alas, I am a queen, not a servant girl. Queens do not perspire. Makarim watches me from across the table, concern written across her features. She thinks I am overcome by the heat. What will she say when I spill out the truth? What will any of them say—here in Jerusalem or at home in Ma'rib?

"She cannot abandon our gods."

"The queen has gone quite mad!"

No. I have not lost my mind. I have found my heart.

I smile at Makarim to assure her all is well. Only this morning she whispered in my ear, "Has the king run away with your affections?"

"Not at all," I insisted and meant it. Solomon already has a thousand women at his beck and call. I see no reason to be counted among them.

The love of a man is no small thing, and the approval of my people is even more dear to me. But I have found something—no, Someone—even more precious.

I turn toward the light streaming between the pillars and lift my arms. Not to call attention to myself but to draw everyone's gaze upward as I prepare to say aloud what I now know is true.

Sheba

Seven

It's
Good
to
Praise God

Praise be to the LORD your God, who has
delighted in you and placed you on the
throne of Israel. Because of the LORD's
eternal love for Israel, he has made you
king to maintain justice and righteousness.

1 KINGS 10:9

Ever since Sheba arrived in Jerusalem, I've been holding my breath, waiting for these words to pour from her lips: "Praise be to the LORD."

Imagine the look on Solomon's face when she spoke God's proper name—twice! *Yahweh. Yahweh.* She acknowledged His reality, His authority, His sovereignty. She commended His love, His power, His truth.

Make no mistake, "the Queen of Sheba was converted."[1] She was God's woman, absolutely.

How can we be sure? Because of the words she said, because only the Holy Spirit could have prompted them, and because of Jesus's admiration for the Queen of the South, recorded in the New Testament.

More on those vital truths in a minute. Sheba is about to make a confession of faith.

"Praise be to the LORD your God, . . ." *1 Kings 10:9*

Glory be, she did it!

With Israel's king as her witness, Sheba embraced the God of Sarah, Rebekah, and Leah, the God of Tamar, Rahab, and Bathsheba. She stepped from the land of the lost into the land of the living, from believing in many gods to believing in the one true God.

Somebody shout, "Hallelujah!"

In her words we hear the jubilance of Moses: "Oh, praise the greatness of our God!"[2] The exuberance of David: "The LORD lives! Praise be to my Rock!"[3] The amazement of Thomas: "My Lord and my God!"[4] And the sheer joy of a new believer publicly confessing her Lord's name, finally grasping who He is.

The Lord. Your God.

YOURS, MINE, OURS

I see you there, raising your hand, wisely pointing out that Sheba said "*your* God," not "*my* God." That's what the original Hebrew says too. The word is masculine and singular. She was talking directly to Solomon. *Your God.*

But the first bit—"Praise be"—in Hebrew means "to kneel, to bless" and is aimed at the Lord alone. Sheba declared, "May the LORD your God be praised" (NET).

In our society we're called to respect those who worship other gods. I do so willingly, but I don't praise their god. I don't bend my knee. Yet Sheba was doing just that. She was praising, she was bending, she was honoring Solomon's God, because He had become *her* God. This wasn't about being socially correct but spiritually direct: "I praise the LORD" (CEV).

Sheba couldn't proclaim such a truth on her own. In the same way that "no one can say, 'Jesus is Lord,' except by the Holy Spirit,"[5] Sheba couldn't say, "Praise God," without divine revelation and sincere dedication. It was God's goodness, rather than Solomon's, that drew Sheba in and won her heart.

This is how it works, beloved. We don't lead people to the Lord. He calls those He loves. It's all His handiwork and all for His glory. In His kindness

God gives us the thrill of witnessing others acknowledge His lordship. It's a life-changing moment for everyone involved, and God alone puts it in motion.

His own Word tells us, "For it is by grace you have been saved, through faith—and this is not from yourselves, it is the gift of God—not by works, so that no one can boast."[6] His grace, salvation, and faith are gifts more precious than all the spices, gold, and jewels in the world.

ALL RISE

The third assurance that Sheba was a child of God? In the New Testament when the Pharisees demanded a sign from Jesus, He responded by commending Sheba, which He never would have done if she were not His own. Jesus said, "The Queen of the South will rise at the judgment with this generation and condemn it."[7] So Sheba will be there when "the Lord himself will come down from heaven, . . . and the dead in Christ will rise first."[8]

The Lord specifically praises Sheba because "she came from the ends of the earth to listen to Solomon's wisdom."[9] That's our girl—a devout seeker of truth. The Pharisees, blinded by their pride, couldn't grasp what Jesus meant by "something greater than Solomon is here."[10] Sheba traveled a long distance to find God, yet these men couldn't identify Him even when He stood in their midst.

Jesus chastised the Pharisees, calling them "hypocrites"[11] and "blind fools"[12] and comparing them to "whitewashed tombs" filled with "everything unclean."[13] We can hear the righteous anger in His voice when He ended His diatribe with "You snakes! You brood of vipers! How will you escape being condemned to hell?"[14]

Oh my.

Jesus held up our Queen of the South as the opposite of these religious men. She sought, she found, she believed. *May the same be said of us, Lord.*

Instead of whitewashed tombs, we want to be daughters of our living God, scrubbed clean and made new, ready to serve.

ON A ROLL

After openly praising God, Sheba honored his servant Solomon.

> ". . . who has delighted in you and placed you
> on the throne of Israel." *1 Kings 10:9*

The Lord has "favored you" (NET), she told Solomon. Sheba wisely saw the blessings and gave credit to the Lord.

I was a slow learner on this one. Used to be when I saw other Christians abundantly blessed with spiritual gifts or material goods, I would praise *them*. I figured they must be doing something right (and I must be doing something wrong). The twin foes of envy and jealousy hounded me, distracted me. Toss in some insecurity and immaturity, and I was pretty much a mess, caught up in the comparison trap and missing the joy of watching God's loving-kindness in action.

Now that enough calendar pages have blown by, I've learned to see blessings for what they are: God being good. God being God. He alone set Solomon on his throne—and Sheba on her throne, for that matter. God blesses whom He chooses, according to His master plan. Our role is to praise Him for that plan, confident we're part of it.

My friend Sheila Walsh once quoted Jeremiah 29:11 from the platform: "'For I know the plans I have for you,' declares the LORD, 'plans to prosper you and not to harm you, plans to give you hope and a future.'" Then Sheila spoke for us all: "Lord, can I just *see* the plans?" Exactly. It's perfectly human to want to know what's next. And perfectly God to say, "Trust Me. I've got this."

Faith means not seeing His plans yet believing they exist.

Hope means not knowing His plans yet trusting the One who designed them.

Love means not understanding His plans yet resting in their goodness.

GOD'S PLAN FOR HIS PEOPLE

Sheba was in Solomon's presence long enough to discern the truth: unlike the gods she feared in her home country, the God of Israel loved His people. While she imagined her false gods threatened, accused, and bedeviled, the God of Israel clearly provided, guided, and protected. The Israelites feared their God because they were in *awe* of Him.

Now Sheba was awestruck as well.

> "Because of the LORD's eternal love
> for Israel, . . ." *1 Kings 10:9*

Love. That's what makes our God so amazing. He loves His people no matter how unlovable we are, and He will do so *forever.* His love is "constant" (EXB) and "unending" (ERV). The sun He placed in the sky rises, then disappears from sight, but not His love. The tides of His oceans ebb and flow but not His love.

Sheba saw God's "desire to uphold them forever"[15] and knew this was no ordinary god. "The LORD will love Israel for all time to come,"[16] she said—as much a prophecy as a proclamation. These were "the people close to his heart,"[17] and Sheba knew He would never let go of them.

He won't let go of you either, dear friend. Take a deep breath and let these comforting truths sink in: *You are loved. You are cherished. You were chosen. You are His.* You belong to the One who said, "Never will I leave you; never will I forsake you."[18]

KING AND QUEEN FOR GOOD REASON

Sheba was still looking at Solomon, all the while praising God.

> "... he has made you king ..." *1 Kings 10:9*

As a monarch, she knew what running a country required. Now she'd discovered the Power behind the throne. Solomon wasn't king because David and Bathsheba wished it so. He was king because God had placed a crown on Solomon's head *before the beginning of time.*

Hard as it is to wrap our heads around this, the Lord "chose us in him before the creation of the world."[19] Long before Genesis 1:1, you and I belonged to God. He created you, claimed you, and gladly "crowns you with love and compassion."[20] He's had a vital purpose in mind all along—for Solomon, for Sheba, and for you.

> "... to maintain justice and righteousness." *1 Kings 10:9*

Because of God's strength, Solomon could "uphold" (CEB) and "administer" (CJB) his kingly task. He could do what was "right and good" (NLV) and "rule fairly and honestly" (CEV). As queens of our own realms, we're called and equipped by God to do likewise. To "be kind and compassionate to one another, forgiving each other, just as in Christ God forgave you."[21]

When God revealed Himself to Sheba, she praised His name. It's a natural response to our supernatural God. What prompts you to praise Him? Something He says in His Word? Something He's done in your life? Something He is?

Our social-media sisters took the challenge and shared the praiseworthy attributes of God that mean the most to them. Among dozens named, here are our top ten:

PRAISE GOD FOR HIS LOVE

Michelle cherishes "His unconditional love, no matter what." The *whats* in her life have been hard. Years apart from the Lord. A husband with a bleeding brain. A young son who committed suicide. And her own stage-four colon cancer. "We ran to God, and His arms were wide open because He loves us. Out of His love come grace and faithfulness, which He has shown us repeatedly."

His Word tells us, "God is love. Whoever lives in love lives in God, and God in them."[22] Of all the times God has demonstrated His love for you, which one produced the greatest sense of gratitude?

PRAISE GOD FOR HIS MERCY

Gena treasures "His mercy. I am a drug addict in recovery and have done so many things I am ashamed of. Even through my time in jail and thoughts of suicide, I realized that God had mercy on my soul. He has carried me out of my misery and shame and brought me to higher ground. I am eternally grateful."

An amazing story, yes? Gena experienced His mercy and so shares her journey without hesitation, urging us to do the same. "Let us then approach God's throne of grace with confidence, so that we may receive mercy."[23]

PRAISE GOD FOR HIS GRACE

Carolyn depends on "His grace. I've made a lot of mistakes, especially recently. But God is right there with me, even through the dark times. He knows I'm a romantic, so when I kept hearing this one love song in my head, I knew it was God calling me back. Still makes me cry to think of it."

His grace not only covers all our stumbling and bumbling. It also opens the doors of heaven for us. "Having been justified by his grace, we might become heirs having the hope of eternal life."[24] Don't worry. *Might* doesn't mean it's up for debate, as in *might* or *might not*. It means we have "come into possession of" (GNT) and "can look forward to" (Phillips) eternal life because God "gave us confidence" (NLT). The original Greek means we can "emerge, become, transition" into our heavenly inheritance, all because of His grace.

PRAISE GOD FOR HIS PRESENCE

A woman named Joy describes how she encountered His presence. "During a very difficult time when I was twelve, God showed me this verse: 'Even if my father and mother abandon me, the LORD will hold me close.'[25] Two years later both my parents did abandon me . . . but God never has. I have experienced His presence my entire life. When I spend time with Him, I always feel that closeness. How awesome is our heavenly Father?!"

Very awesome.

In the early days of the church, Peter was prompted by the Holy Spirit to visit Cornelius, who assured Peter, "We are all here in the presence of God."[26] His presence isn't just a nebulous concept; it's a here-and-now reality we can experience firsthand.

PRAISE GOD FOR HIS PATIENCE

Michelle favors the classic word that describes God's patience: long-suffering. "It's been twenty-five years since I challenged God on His promise 'I have overcome the world.'[27] I loved God, then fought God, then trusted Him, then (un)trusted Him—you get the picture. Through my struggle to believe He is truly a God that has overcome this wretched world, His long-suffering love healed me."

The Lord also "waited patiently in the days of Noah"[28] while His servant found the wood, constructed the ark, and loaded the animals. The whole process must have taken forever (or seemed like it to Noah, at least). The Greek word translated "patiently" or "long-suffering" is really two words meaning "long" plus "anger." So long-suffering is the opposite of being short-tempered. Good thing our God has patience in abundance!

PRAISE GOD FOR HIS FAITHFULNESS

Wanda clings to the promise of His faithfulness. "My husband and I are in pastoral ministry. Many times there hasn't been enough paycheck to cover all the bills, and yet we always have what we need. Our motto is 'The Father has provided again.' God is indeed faithful!"

Yes, He is. This is one of the aspects of God's nature that means the most to me and to many of our sisters:

"I cling to His faithfulness like a lifeline."—Donnalee

"No matter what I've been through, He comes through."—Esther

"When others abandon me, when I abandon myself, He remains."—Kristi

"I fail Him every day, and yet He is still with me and for me!"—Sally

King David praised Him with these words: "Your love, LORD, reaches to the heavens, your faithfulness to the skies."[29] Above the cares of this world, beyond the sin that entangles us, past the limits of our understanding—we can't begin to touch the outer reaches of His great faithfulness.

PRAISE GOD FOR HIS FORGIVENESS

Pam is astounded by the breadth of His forgiveness. "My earthly father couldn't or wouldn't forgive me, so I didn't believe my heavenly Father could and would forgive me for anything, let alone everything. I wasted a lot of years away from God because I thought I was unforgivable."

That's why Paul (and every preacher since) has declared, "My friends, I want you to know that through Jesus the forgiveness of sins is proclaimed to you."[30] We need to hear this good news again and again before the truth can cut through our unbelief, our stubbornness, our pain and finally settle into our hearts.

PRAISE GOD FOR HIS STEADFASTNESS

Cara delights in His steadfastness. "How impossible it would be to serve a God who changes His mind! Instead, He is always the same. He is always good." Jan agrees: "So comforting to know He does not, will not, cannot change in a world that changes constantly." And Dawn rests in the fact that "He is constant. He is the great I AM. Always has been, always will be."

The truth that calms my heart on a daily basis? "Jesus Christ is the same yesterday and today and forever."[31] Whatever changes in life we might face, our God never changes.

Kristi also marvels at His loyalty. "No matter what I have done (a lot) or where I have gone (very far), He is still there. While I have been pursuing other idols, He has continued to pursue me. He is loyal beyond understanding."

PRAISE GOD FOR BEING OUR FATHER

Robin admits, "He is the Daddy I have longed for my whole life. He fills all my empty places with His love. Through His Word He teaches me everything I need to know. He comforts me, letting me pour out my heart to Him. He never grows tired of my persistence or frustrated with my slowness. He is wise to discipline me when I need it. He is faithful to do what He promises, so I can totally trust Him. God is a good Father."

Our earthly fathers may do their best, but no man, however godly, can manage all the above. What a relief—for them and for us—to have a heavenly Father who cares for His children.

PRAISE GOD FOR HIS SOVEREIGNTY

Marcia stakes her faith in His sovereignty. Through the death of her mother, a son in prison, and the betrayal of a friend, Marcia learned, "He can be trusted to do what is best even when it doesn't seem so at the time." Christine agrees: "Knowing that God is in control is a great comfort to me."

Anytime I lose sight of just how truly powerful God is, I read four short chapters in Scripture, Job 38–41, which open with God's thunderous challenge to Job: "Where were you when I laid the earth's foundation?"[32] This passage is so familiar at the Higgs house, all we have to say is "Where were you?" and a healthy fear of the Lord quickly stirs in our hearts.

Would the queen of Sheba have praised God for His love, mercy, and grace? His presence, patience, and faithfulness? His forgiveness, steadfastness, and fatherliness? Given time, she no doubt discovered all those attributes and more.

But in this moment she praised God for His sovereignty. She knew He'd appointed King Solomon to his throne and had blessed him with wisdom beyond human understanding. Sheba saw with her own eyes the power of the Almighty. No wonder she burst into praise!

ME? I PRAISE GOD FOR HIS LIGHT

Like Sheba, I did not acknowledge the one true God for many years and instead lived in darkness. Led astray by foolish ideas and blinded by selfish desires, I spent most of my twenties in shadowy nightclubs and bars, looking for love and settling for less. Much less.

It was easier to live in the dark than to step into the light and face the truth about myself. But God, the Source of Light, did not give up on me.

That husband-and-wife team He sent into my workplace? They were positively *filled* with light. Their eyes shone like stars, and their faces were radiant. I'm not kidding. These two people? They *glowed*.

Monday through Friday they brought a Bible to work. (I'm not sure that was legal even back then!) In the break room they read passages aloud, then discussed them—as if the words were important, as if they made a difference.

When I heard "Light has come into the world, but people loved darkness instead of light because their deeds were evil,"[33] I was sure they were talking about me. Even so, I was drawn to them. Or maybe it was the light inside them or the warmth of their hugs. All I know is, I couldn't turn away.

They made me welcome in their home and in their lives. They taught me what they sincerely believed to be true and showed me a God who promised to banish the darkness.

One day He did. It was like turning on a floor lamp in a darkened room. No light? Light everywhere. No truth? Truth everywhere.

All the words my friends had been pouring into me suddenly made sense.

It wasn't because of anything I did, believe me. I was still smoking pot, drinking Southern Comfort, and sleeping around with men I hardly knew.

I was a mess.

In the midst of all my sin, God broke through. He aimed the beacon of His grace at the darkest corners of my soul. Not to shame me, but to claim me. Not to put an end to me, but to give me a new beginning.

God soon revealed why He'd rescued me from the deepest, darkest pit: so His Son would be glorified. The spotlight is always meant to fall on Christ, not on Christians. On the Savior, not on the saved.

It's taken me thirty years to understand this.

"God once said, 'Let the light shine out of the darkness!' This is the same

God who made his light shine in our hearts by letting us know the glory of God that is in the face of Christ."[34]

Three thousand years ago Sheba saw the Light.

Her first instinct was the right one: to call Him Lord and praise His holy name.

*F*rom the steps of the palace courtyard, I wave forward the first gift bearers, watching King Solomon's rugged features soften as each treasure chest is laid open at his feet.

The gold catches the fire of the sun. The jewels wink at him, coy as maidens. But it is the amber-colored frankincense that draws his gaze. He reaches down to touch the resin, then rubs the waxy residue between his fingers, his smile broadening.

Solomon is pleased. And I sense God is pleased as well.

God. It will take time for me to envision One rather than dozens.

Will the Almighty speak to me as He speaks to Solomon? Can I know Him in the same intimate way even though I fear Him? I have much to learn. Each hour with Solomon has been worth our long journey here. He has advised me, "Walk with the wise and become wise."[1] If the gods— No, if *God* allows, I will continue growing in His wisdom when I return home.

The camels hold up their heads, defying the heat, ignoring the pesky flies. Draped across them are luxurious carpets woven by our best artisans. Alimah leads her troupe of dancers through the courtyard, and Shadiyah fills the air with her sweet voice.

Pride wells inside me as Solomon admires the best our country has to offer. He will not soon forget us. I brought more than custom required—and far more than my advisors recommended. Watching the parade of riches passing before us now, I am glad I trusted my own opinion.

A queen can never be too generous, too gracious, too kind. In Solomon's words, "A kindhearted woman gains honor."[2] The sort of honor, he says, that cannot be sought or bought. Only bestowed by God.

A trio of silk banners flutter through the air, marking the end of the procession of gifts. A handful of sunsets remain before we begin our journey south. I glance at Solomon. Will he miss my company? I confess, I will dearly miss his. But I have met His God and am comforted, knowing He will never depart from my side.

Sheba

Eight

It's
Good
to
Give
Generously

And she gave the king 120 talents of
gold, large quantities of spices, and
precious stones. Never again were so
many spices brought in as those the
queen of Sheba gave to King Solomon.

1 KINGS 10:10

Rather than presenting all her riches to Solomon when she first arrived in Jerusalem, Sheba waited until the high point of their visit—*after* she'd tested his wisdom, *after* he'd answered her many questions, and *after* she'd embraced his God.

At last she was ready to express her gratitude with an impressive array of parting gifts. Solomon knew this stash of goodies was on standby. But in the ancient world, there was a proper time for exchanging diplomatic gifts between royals.

The moment had come.

And she gave the king 120 talents of gold, . . . *1 Kings 10:10*

My favorite translation? "Gold weighing as much as 120 small men" (NLV). *Really* small men since a talent weighed only about seventy-five pounds![3] Still, any way you weigh it, "4½ tons" (ERV) or "nine thousand pounds" (EXB) of gold is a staggering sum.

. . . large quantities of spices, and precious stones. *1 Kings 10:10*

Oh yes, we remember. Sheba brought a "huge amount" (CJB) of "sweet smelling things" (WYC), plus "sack after sack of . . . expensive gems" (MSG). But it was her aromatic offerings that made the greatest impression. Rare and precious in any kingdom, these spices from the land of Sheba were the most personal and the most prized of her gifts. In fact, the people of Israel had never seen such a load of balsam, myrrh, Arabian balm, and frankincense enter their country—nor would they witness it a second time.

> Never again were so many spices brought in as those the
> queen of Sheba gave to King Solomon. *1 Kings 10:10*

"Abundance" (ESV) is the word scholars have used over the centuries to describe Sheba's "cargo of spices" (MSG), a quantity that has "never been matched" (NET).

We can only imagine the number of limestone jars filled with liquid balsam, a pure sap drawn from the *opobalsamum* tree. Myrrh resin, harvested from small, thorny *myrrha* trees, would have been offered to Solomon in great sacks, the yellowish gum turned hard and glossy. Frankincense, traded across the Arabian Peninsula for two thousand years before Sheba's time, was harvested by slashing the bark of *Boswellia* trees and catching the dripping resin called tears.[4]

The cost is incalculable, but this much we know: Arabian spices were worth far more than gold. When it comes to being generous, Sheba set a high standard.

WHAT CAN A MODERN SPICE
GIRL OFFER?

If we can't give friends and loved ones extravagant gifts like Sheba's, what do we give them? Brenda admitted, "I pray before buying a gift. Okay, so I'm weird." Not at all weird, sister. If we pray before we eat, why not pray before we shop? The way Elizabeth sees it, "Giving a gift feels like partnering with God to bless another person."

When I asked women what they love to give, their answers fell into four basic categories. See if any of these are your favorites.

Money has several pluses. No expiration date. No need for returns or exchanges. No concerns about fit, color, or style. Whether to tuck a check, cash, or a gift card in the envelope is the only real issue. Gwen admits, "I have friends who insist gift cards are the way to go, but in my mind that's almost as bad as no gift at all! No thought, no emotional connection!"

Call me crazy, but I love gift cards from a favorite store, a movie theater, or a restaurant. Any amount of cash that lands outside the family budget? Most welcome.

Stuff is nice too. Jewelry, accessories—all that. Melissa reminds us, "Even the smallest thing can brighten someone's day." And Debbie says, "I love it when I find the One Thing that is totally that person."

Last December I bought tall wooden letters for my husband, spelling out the three words he often includes in the signature of his e-mails—*Soli Deo Gloria,* Latin for "Glory to God Alone." Not only is my Bill a language geek, but this phrase is one of the five *solas* that summarize the basic tenets of the Reformation. To get the most mileage out of his gift, I wrapped the letters in random pairs and scattered them around the tree.

On Christmas morning Bill opened one package, then another, looking more confused by the minute. He stood the letters side by side on a nearby table, moving them around to create different possibilities. SOLID EGO? I assured him it was *not* that. OGRE DOLLS? Not this Christmas.

With each new letter the what-does-this-spell mystery deepened. Everyone joined in, trying to guess. GOOD LIARS? Nice try.

"Wait!" our son burst out. "I think it's something about glory—"

I watched my husband's expression change as realization sank in.

"Soli Deo Gloria," Bill finally said, rearranging the letters, tears in his eyes. "Best gift ever, Liz."

My favorite present that year? His joy. Because the sweetest gift has no price tag.

Maybe that's why *homemade treasures* are another favorite among gift givers. As Jan says, "Even if it's just a pie made from scratch, it's from the heart." Hannah likes making handmade presents "because I can pray for the person as I'm working."

One gift that costs nothing actually costs us the most: *time.* Sheila believes in giving "acts of love and service," and Linda's presents are "spending time with a friend, cleaning her house, providing a meal, watching her children." (Sorry, I do not have Linda's phone number.) Angela reminds us, "The best gift comes from a heart of self-sacrifice."

In the end gift giving is about deepening our relationships. Sheba's gifts for Solomon were a clear statement of her respect and admiration for him. Her generosity ensured he would never forget her.

MOTIVE MATTERS

Surrounded with gemstones, the king no doubt expressed his thanks: "Best agates ever, Sheba." Something like that. Royal visitors were known to come bearing gifts in one hand while holding out the other, expecting something in return. In Solomon's words, "Many curry favor with a ruler, and everyone is the friend of one who gives gifts."[5]

What inspired Sheba to be so generous? In part, she was reimbursing her host for the cost of her visit, but she was also extending a hand of friendship and blessing a man who had abundantly blessed her.

When I asked our sisters what prompts them to be generous, one recurring answer surprised me. "I get pleasure from giving," one woman said. Another confessed, "It definitely benefits me more than them." A third declared, "Giving makes me happy!"

Wait. Isn't gift giving about making *other* people happy?

As more responses rolled in, I realized it was perfectly natural to feel good about helping other people feel good. Doesn't His Word tell us, "Good will come to those who are generous"?[6] It would be downright sad if giving made you feel bad!

Sheba must have taken great pleasure in presenting all her lavish gifts to Solomon. After all, giving blesses both ways. It's a conversation, not a monologue.

For Marie, "Seeing someone smile is like receiving a gift myself." And for Norma, "The look on their faces? Priceless!" Recalling Bill's expression last Christmas, I totally agree. Shelly adds, "Giving is a way of cleansing your life from 'selfie mode.'" Heaven knows, we all need that. And Kathy has learned, "I feel my best when I am helping someone else. It is what we are here for." Yes, it is.

IT'S ABOUT BLESSING OTHERS

Some of our sisters are motivated to give because, as Theresa admits, we "know what it's like *not* to get." Jonna looks for opportunities "to brighten the life of a shut-in," and Luci has compassion for seniors since "so many are alone." Helping others who are less fortunate, who would never ask for help, who have no way of reciprocating—these generous acts bring us closer to the One who gave His all for us.

Gifts speak a language all their own. A woman named Esther believes they help us "move beyond the superficial chatter to being able to say—albeit often without words—'You matter. I see you. I hear you. I care.'" Recipients feel noticed, remembered, thought about, wanted, appreciated, loved.

Cheryl's motivation might be the best of all: "I give out of gratitude."

GIVING WITHOUT FEAR

Jesus gave everything He had so we could have everything He came to give. The freedom of forgiveness. The grace to begin afresh every morning. The promise of eternal life. When we give to others, we do so in His name and because of His example.

"God says to give," Judy reminds us, "and I want to please Him." She's right. Scripture calls us "to be rich in good deeds, and to be generous and willing to share."[7] As Angela says, "In a world that is so self-absorbed and constantly focused on what we can get, we're called to a different mind-set."

I agree with absolutely everything I've shared here about giving: my words, your words, God's Word. Now the truth: *I am not doing all of it*. Not by a long shot.

Oh, I gladly hand out money to loved ones and am willing to buy them presents—*if* they give me a wish list and *if* I can order everything online. That's not being kind; it's being efficient. When it comes to blessing people, *efficiency* is not a virtue.

Have I given loved ones what they've wanted? Sure. Have my gifts deepened our relationships? Not nearly as much as two hours around the dinner table playing Bananagrams.

What about handmade gifts? No talent. Not happening.

Cleaning houses, doing laundry, baking casseroles, or doing any other generous act of service? No time. Not happening.

What's going on here? Selfishness, for starters, but it goes deeper than that.

It's fear. Fear of failing, of disappointing, of not getting it right. Fear of putting a wrinkle in our relationship. Fear that if I choose the wrong gift, someone won't think well of me. Fear that if I spend too much, I'll offend or embarrass. Fear that if I spend too little, I'll hurt the person's feelings.

If any of these fears strike a chord with you, here's another take on gift giving, meant to set us all free. "The *real* gift," Colleen says, "is letting others know God cares about them." *Boom*. It's not about us *or* the gift. It's about loving God and loving people with our whole hearts.

Rather than fretting "Will they like my present?" the question we need to ask is "How can I demonstrate God's generous love and abundant compassion to the world around me?"

RIGHT PRESENT, WRONG PERSON

Even given as a token of God's love, a gift can land in the wrong hands. Mine, for example.

Two dozen springs ago I spoke at a luncheon decorated with beautiful silk flowers. An enthusiastic woman stepped forward to tell me she'd designed the arrangements herself, then handed me one to take home. I thanked her profusely as we headed for the door.

I found the perfect place for the flowers, but the milk-glass vase wasn't a good fit for our décor. Replacing it with a simple basket, I tossed the vase in the kitchen trash can and forgot all about it.

Two days later the phone rang. "Remember the floral arrangement I gave you?" The woman was almost gasping for air. "You're welcome to keep the flowers, but that vase is a valuable antique of my mother's. She just called to ask if I'd seen it. Would you mind sending it back?"

Mind? Friend, my mind was blank. *What did I do with her vase?*

"H-happy to return it," I stammered, "but it may take me a few days to find . . . uh, just the right box." I jotted down her address, hung up the phone, and began tearing our kitchen apart, praying like a madwoman.

Retracing my steps from the moment The Vase entered the house, I soon realized where it had landed.

I am a blessed and grateful woman. The trash bags were still by the curb. Her milk glass was no worse for wear and was soon reunited with its rightful owner. When the woman called back to thank me, she apologized again and again, which only made me feel worse.

"Shall I find another milk-glass vase for you?"

"No! No, really. The basket I have is . . . perfect."

God brings this story to mind every time I'm tempted to ask someone, "So are you using that _____ I gave you?" Some questions are best left unsaid. We're meant to give out of love, not out of expectation. If our gift is enjoyed and appreciated, wonderful. If it's regifted or sold on eBay or dropped in a box for Goodwill, that doesn't change the value of our gift.

It's not the thought that counts. It's the love that counts.

A GIFT FIT FOR A KING (OR QUEEN)

Everything Sheba presented to Solomon was extravagantly beautiful and imminently useful. Just for fun, I asked women what sort of hostess gift they might present to, say, Queen Elizabeth II.

> "A linen guest towel with 'My home is my castle.'"—Suzanne
> "Saltwater taffy from the Jersey Shore."—Donna
> "Organic dog biscuits for the corgis."—Carolyn
> "Tupperware."—Denise
> "A live chicken. Like peasants brought when they visited the
> king."—Donna

These women are fearless about their royal gift giving. Next we'll find out if Solomon was equally brave when he offered the queen of Sheba his parting gift.

Considering her wealth, her position, and the exalted circles she traveled in, Sheba might have been difficult to impress. But a woman who is truly generous extends more than her coin purse. She is also generous with her heart, her knowledge, her calendar, her experience, and her willingness to receive gifts from others—whatever those presents might be.

Of all Sheba's fine attributes, that's the one I most need to learn.

Solomon thinks my gifts are too generous. I can see it in the way he stands with his weight shifted onto his back foot, putting a slight distance between us.

Even so, I do not regret one talent of gold, one handful of myrrh. Solomon has shared things of far greater value. Wisdom surpassing the bounds of human knowledge. Faith in the one true God, who rules over all His creation. What gifts, however grand, can match these?

I ignore the sand rubbing my skin raw beneath the straps of my sandals and stand as tall as I can, wanting to convey my regal authority. These are the riches of a queen I am laying before him, not love trinkets from a woman bent on wooing the king. It is imperative that Solomon—and, more so, his governors—clearly see my intentions.

I have come to give, not to take. To bless the king, not to burden him with expectations. If a trade agreement comes from our visit, it must be honestly won.

He stands so near that I clasp my hands lest I reach out to touch him and assure him my bounty is freely given. When Solomon turns toward me, his gaze is considerably warmer, as if he felt the imaginary brush of my fingers on his sleeve.

His smile is genuine. His gratitude is sincere. His appeal—it must be said—is almost irresistible. A weaker woman might be tempted. But I have never been called weak.

Still, when he looks at me this way, when he asks, "What is your desire, O Queen?" I swallow hard and remember Solomon cautioning his sons about "the wayward woman with her seductive words."[1]

By the strength of this God who has claimed my heart, that woman will not be me.

Not this day. Not ever.

Sheba

Nine

It's
Good
to
Receive
Graciously

King Solomon gave the queen of Sheba
all she desired and asked for, besides what
he had given her out of his royal bounty.

1 KINGS 10:13

Now we come to the verse that has launched a thousand legends, from salacious stories in the fourteenth century to twentieth-century movie posters shouting, "Behold! The love story of the ages!"[2]

For some the question remains: Did the relationship between Solomon and Sheba move beyond respect, beyond friendship, beyond mutual admiration? Did they in fact become lovers? Newlyweds? Parents to a prince?

As I said at the start, you and I are sticking to God's Word. But over the centuries not everyone has done so. Sheba's story "lit up the imaginations of those around her—and the fires still burn."[3]

The Kabbalah calls her Lilith, a demon in Jewish folklore. In the Middle Ages her story turned more magical in one of the revered books of the Islamic world, *Tales of the Prophets.* In those accounts she has a human father and a djinn for a mother, plus outrageously hairy legs, and a misshapen left foot, webbed like a goose's foot or cloven like a goat's hoof.

Oh my.

Another document, the *Kebra Nagast,* a holy book for Ethiopian Christians compiled in the fourteenth century, reveals the story of Menelik— "Son of the Wise"—founder of an Ethiopian empire that lasted almost to the end of the twentieth century. His father, according to legend? King Solomon. And his mother? Makeda, also known as—that's right—the queen of Sheba.

A mix of resources from several cultures combined to create Menelik's story, held dear by the people of Ethiopia.[4] But the *Kebra Nagast* travels far beyond the biblical account to create an entirely separate historical tradition for Sheba,[5] encompassing both sides of the Red Sea.

Could the land of Sheba have included South Arabia *and* Ethiopia? Yes, it's possible. The two regions are separated by nothing more than a narrow body of water, and "ethnically they were closely related."[6] But the tradition that the Ethiopian royal line descended directly from Solomon and Sheba "is difficult to substantiate."[7]

Where does that leave our queen? Safely preserved in God's Word. Older than any of the other resources mentioned here, the Bible gives us the real Sheba, without embellishment.

So did she or did she not give birth to Solomon's son?

The answer is waiting for us.

GIVE THE WOMAN WHAT SHE WANTS

> King Solomon gave the queen
> of Sheba . . . *1 Kings 10:13*

After all, she'd given first. Now it was his turn. Nothing unusual, just diplomatic protocol. The Hebrew word *nathan*—yes, like the popular name—is translated as "gave" here and can also mean "to put, set." We find no hidden meanings, no euphemisms, no whispered gossip, no suggestive language.

Solomon *gave*. Period. And what was his present?

> . . . all she desired . . . *1 Kings 10:13*

True, a word like *desire* is rife with possibilities. But the Hebrew, *chephets*, doesn't point to anything physical or sexual. It simply means "delight." Something that's "acceptable" or "valuable," something that "matters" and has "purpose."[8]

We already know the one thing Sheba wanted most: "She came from the ends of the earth to listen to Solomon's wisdom."[9] Nowhere in Scripture are we told she desired the king's company in her bed or wished for his child in her womb as a parting gift. Nor does it say Solomon knew her or lay with her or any other roundabout way of implying he made love to her.

Nevertheless, more than one writer has leaped to that assumption, declaring "the son of Solomon . . . was born to the Queen of Sheba from her desire . . . for every princess of that day was anxious to become one of his wives."[10] A princess, still under her father's guiding hand, might wish to be counted among Solomon's seven hundred wives. But a reigning queen would never choose to bear a son for a distant monarch and risk losing her throne.

JUST SAYING

I won't jump on my soapbox for long, but I confess, I'm weary of scholars, interpreters, and commentators—male *and* female—reducing commendable women in Scripture to prostitutes, adulteresses, and mere objects of male desire.

Ruth did *not* seduce Boaz when she visited him at the threshing floor at midnight.

Mary Magdalene did *not* have an improper relationship with Jesus, let alone with a long line of male customers before Him.

And Sheba did *not* marry, sleep with, or provide an heir for King Solomon.

Nothing in the original Hebrew or Greek or in any ancient historical records supports these myths. Still, they continue to circulate, in part because women are often wrongly viewed as flirtatious, sensuous, even downright dangerous, especially those women whom God has given a leading role.

Like Ruth, whose exemplary story of redemption fills an entire book of the Bible.

Like Mary Magdalene, who beheld the risen Christ and was sent by Him to share the news with His disciples.

Like Sheba, sovereign over tens of thousands, who went to Jerusalem for wisdom and embraced its heavenly Source.

These women may or may not have been easy on the eyes, but this is certain: their appearance is never noted and their actions are never questioned within Scripture. Do we find alluring yet morally reprehensible women in the Bible? Of course. But these three, and many others, don't qualify.

The truth is, Solomon met Sheba's "every desire"[11] soon after she arrived. Once she'd shared "all that she had on her mind,"[12] Solomon swiftly "answered all her questions."[13] *All* of them. Done.

Her desires had been met. Her mission accomplished. And when she sang out, "Praise be to the LORD,"[14] her heart was filled to overflowing.

As for Solomon giving presents to Sheba, they were "gifts he would have given any other ruler."[15] Nothing shocking or immoral happened during their gift exchange. Solomon didn't carry her off to his chamber, then whisper lines from the Song of Songs in the gentle curve of her ear, as we see in the Technicolor spectacle *Solomon and Sheba*.

The real queen of Sheba is worthy of our respect, despite what artists have painted and Hollywood has tainted and poets like William Butler Yeats have written:

Sang Solomon to Sheba,
And kissed her Arab eyes,
"There's not a man or woman
Born under the skies

Dare match in learning with us two,
And all day long we have found
There's not a thing but love can make
The world a narrow pound."[16]

I enjoy a good love story as much as the next person, but we do our biblical sisters a disservice when we turn their heroic journeys into steamy romances, ignoring their deep love for God in favor of titillating rumors of forbidden sex.

At least one contemporary author turned down the heat on this "all she desired" business: "It is much more likely that the phrase simply reflects that the visit was successful, and the desired treaties were executed."[17] That's our role model, doing her royal duty. Go, Sheba.

Soapbox dismounted. Back to our story.

THE BIG ASK

. . . and asked for, . . . *1 Kings 10:13*

Sheba clearly let her wishes be known. Was she being pushy? Presumptuous? Not according to God's Word. We're urged to boldly state what we want, confident of His response—*if* our desire reflects His desire for us.

The book of James tells us, "If any of you lacks wisdom, you should ask God, who gives generously to all without finding fault, and it will be given to you."[18] That was precisely Sheba's experience. She sought wisdom—first from Solomon, then from his God—and graciously received what she'd asked for.

The same is true for us. If we pray according to His Word and His will, we can count on a positive response. The timing is His alone, but the assurance stands: "Ask and it will be given to you."[19] Not it *might* be given. It *will* be given.

God has made the request process as easy as possible. "Ask the LORD your God for a sign."[20] "Ask the LORD for rain in the springtime."[21] "Ask the Lord of the harvest . . . to send out workers."[22]

We get it, Lord. *Ask.*

Want a few tips on how to ask? "In every situation, by prayer and petition, with thanksgiving, present your requests to God."[23] *Anytime, anywhere?* You bet. *Pray?* Sure. *Present?* Can do. *Request?* On it.

Now look what's quietly tucked in the middle: *with thanksgiving.* God wants us to be grateful even before we ask and even before He answers. To pray, fully believing and thanking Him in advance. To receive both expectantly and graciously those things we've asked for.

When a Canaanite woman pleaded with Jesus to have mercy on her demon-possessed daughter, she asked Him three times, convinced the Lord alone could set her girl free. Finally Jesus told her, "Woman, you have great faith! Your request is granted." The result? "Her daughter was healed at that moment."[24]

We ask because we believe, and we believe because He answers. Our faith grows with every ask, every seek, every knock. "How much more will your Father in heaven give good gifts to those who ask him!"[25]

Whatever Sheba asked of King Solomon, he gave her even more, following the example of the Lord himself.

ABOVE AND BEYOND

. . . besides what he had given her out
of his royal bounty. 1 Kings 10:13

In addition to "all the customary gifts he had so generously given" (NLT), he dug into his own pockets, "his own personal funds" (CEB), to honor the queen of Sheba with "his royal riches" (NIrV).

We know the Lord is behind this, generously blessing Sheba through Solomon's abundant wealth. As Solomon recorded, "Those who find me"—meaning wisdom—"find life and receive favor from the LORD."[26]

Eternal life is gift enough. But God doesn't stop there. He favors, blesses, and enriches those who seek Him. The One who is "able to do immeasurably more than all we ask or imagine"[27] made certain Sheba's camels were heaped with Israel's best offerings that day in Jerusalem.

How did Sheba receive those gifts? Very well, it seems. We have no record of her protesting, "Oh no! I couldn't possibly take all this." No resistance on her part, no false modesty, no cries of "Sol, you shouldn't have!" Sheba not only gave generously; she also received graciously.

GETTING PERSONAL

Now the embarrassing truth: I enjoy giving, but I'm not really good at receiving, especially if it's an act of service. When I mentioned this online and asked for suggestions about learning to accept gifts more graciously, the response was swift and occasionally sharp (ouch).

One woman wrote, "Let others do for you and act happy about it. Otherwise, you are just being incredibly rude." Wow, did *that* get my attention. "We need to let others be a blessing and not try to take all the glory of giving for ourselves." Oh dear. Is that what I'm doing? "When we refuse help from others, we are joy stealers," another woman cautioned. "God and I had a little chat about my attitude," she added. "Take my advice before He chats with you too."

Actually, God has been chatting with me nonstop since I asked the question, gently prying me open with His Word. We're meant to be a grateful people, "always giving thanks to God the Father for everything."[28] Sheba, new to the faith, understood the Source of her gifts and received them with joy. Why can't I, a seasoned believer, do the same?

I found myself scrolling through the responses, hoping to find lots of other women who share my challenge. There are a few of us. A very few.

Moira admits, "I find it harder to accept gifts than to give them, and I think it's because of my 'I can do it myself' attitude. The Lord often reminds me that I *can't*." Right there on the same square, sister.

Patti has my number when she points out, "Giving is more about control than receiving is. We need to let go." *Uh-oh*. I also identify with Pam, who says, "I am very independent and want to give, not get." Guilty as charged.

Finally I read Ginny's confession and was undone: "When I refuse or balk at receiving a blessing, I'm insulting God, since He's the ultimate giver." Friend, I do *not* want to go there.

THE HEART OF THE MATTER

Mary's brief comment showed me what's really going on: "I love to give— and find it harder to receive. Probably a pride issue."

Sigh. Yes, it probably is.

Cathy remembers a time when family medical bills were mounting and a paycheck-to-paycheck friend handed over her Christmas-club check. Cathy says that when she tried to push it back across the table, "My friend placed her hands on mine and said, 'God told me to give it to you. It's not mine anymore; it's yours.' Her love pushed my pride out of the way."

"Pride is a very sneaky thing," Laura says, "especially when it comes in the form of false humility, saying things like 'I'm fine' or 'I don't have any needs.'" Been there, sisters. And I smiled at Michele's take: "Nope, just let me continue to appear to be awesome without your help."

So how can we learn to receive gifts as graciously as Sheba—with open hands and open hearts and genuine gratitude? Here are some new ways of looking at life on the receiving end.

RECEIVING IS A FORM OF GIVING

When Marsha went through a season of receiving after her daughter's car accident, she admits, "It was difficult. But I noticed relief on the face of each person from whom I accepted help. I could see how therapeutic it was for them. By receiving, we're giving people a chance to be the blessing they want to be."

Leslie believes, "Your smile, your gratitude, your kind words give back to the giver something that is worth more than gold: the sense that the gift has been accepted and has value." And Debi reminds us to "think of sweet acceptance and appreciation as yet another gift you can give."

So I'll still be giving even when I'm receiving? That helps.

People *do* like to see where their gifts land. When a friend presented me with a handmade quilt (be still, my heart), I hurried home, hung it on my dining room wall, snapped a picture with my phone, and texted her immediately with the photo and my deepest thanks. (It's still hanging there, Cindy. Beautiful as ever.) Though I couldn't possibly match her generosity, I wanted some way to bless her in return.

RECEIVING IS NECESSARY

Eveline reminds us, "'God loves a cheerful giver,'[29] which means we need some cheerful takers." She has a point.

Valerie agrees: "If everyone refused to accept gifts, whom could the givers give to?" Sounds like a scene worthy of *The Twilight Zone,* with every person in town walking around like robots, arms outstretched, offering gifts no one can receive because their hands are already full.

"Give, and it will be given to you," the Bible tells us. "A good measure, pressed down, shaken together and running over."[30] If we give, we have to be ready to receive.

RECEIVING MEANS FOCUSING ON THE GIVER

Emily speaks for many of us: "I hate to say it, but I typically don't want more stuff, so that's part of the problem." I so get that. When we focus on the gift instead of the giver, we miss the party. Gifts aren't about *what;* they're about *who.* The other person is all that truly matters.

Dody understands this. "Our minds need to be focused on the giver—on her joy, fulfillment, and excitement—and not on how we feel as receivers." Talk about an aha! I love making other people happy. If I think of receiving as another way to bless someone, I can avoid being incredibly rude (please, Lord) and make the giver feel fabulous.

When Carol helped her mom downsize and move into a small condo, she put a ton of miles on her car and had to reschedule her family and work life. "We did a lot of restaurant eating on those day trips," she admitted. "Mom insisted on paying for our meals, but one time I just couldn't let her pay yet again. 'Let me do this,' she insisted. 'No, Mom, it's fine,' I responded. 'I've got it.' Then I looked up and saw her tears. 'Please,' she said, dabbing her cheeks, 'let me pay. It's the only thing I can do anymore.' I learned a valuable lesson that day about recognizing another person's dignity and her right to contribute in meaningful ways."

RECEIVING IS A FORM OF GRACE

Grace? It's my favorite subject to speak about, write about, sing about, blog about, "to the praise of his glorious grace, which he has freely given us in the One he loves."[31]

But I hadn't considered how *receiving* might fall under the broad umbrella of God's unmerited favor. Desiree believes it does. "Salvation is a gift we humbly receive. We should also graciously receive the gifts that God gives us through others. It's all about grace."

The lovely Greek word *charis* means "grace, kindness." It's what saves us, sustains us, surrounds us, secures us. Again, that favorite verse: "For it is by grace you have been saved, through faith—and this is not from yourselves, it is the gift of God."[32] But that gift, that *dóron* in Greek, specifically means a "sacrifice." It's a present we can never hope to match. We can only accept it, embrace it, receive it.

Moe's story begins with an honest confession: "I spent a couple of months on welfare and food stamps. One Sunday the preacher took me aside and presented me with a box of food the church had collected and an envelope of cash. I was ashamed and humiliated! But God took me aside as well. Yes, someone has to be the receiver, but I think it goes deeper than that. It's how God trains us. Unless we've been there, how can we relate to the poor family that really needs our help but doesn't want charity?"

Charity. *Charis.* Grace.

RECEIVING TEACHES US HUMILITY

Joan believes, "Gratitude is humbling. We must accept it."

I'm noting a pattern here. God is at work in us, molding us, stretching us. Asking hard things of us. To receive when we'd rather give. To accept when we're rather refuse.

As Wendy sees it, "When we reject people's gifts of time, resources, hugs, and other treasures, we block the method that God uses to speak to us, heal us, invite us, revive us, and rewire us to send us out for more effective ministry." Five great reasons to receive with gladness and gratitude.

Because God "shows favor to the humble,"[33] the gifts of grace He showers on His children are experienced in greater measure by those who humbly receive. Jeanie learned this firsthand. "One day I had a life of plenty and did all the giving, and the next day it was all gone. If it hadn't been for the love and generosity of my friends and family, my children and I wouldn't have survived. Was it easy? No! But God humbled me and showed me that others needed the blessing of helping me."

RECEIVING MEANS ACKNOWLEDGING YOUR WORTH

I didn't see this one coming. Diane gently suggests, "Not feeling worthy might be the core of your dilemma, Liz."

Wait. I thought my *pride* was the problem. Well, yes, that too.

"For me," Amanda says, "it boils down to a strange mixture of being too proud to be grateful and feeling unworthy of the gesture or gift." Who knew we could feel prideful and unworthy at the same time? Is there a pill for that? A support group? Something?!

No, but there's hope. Diana affirms, "God is teaching me that I am worthy."

RECEIVING GRACIOUSLY HONORS THE LORD

What a relief to shine the spotlight now on the One who is *most* worthy—to make it all about Him and not about us. Susan challenges us to "receive each gift as if it's from God, because it is!" His Word makes that abundantly clear: "Every good and perfect gift is from above, coming down from the Father of the heavenly lights."[34]

The most perfect gift is His Son. As Debrah says, "If I accepted the ultimate gift of Jesus without reservation, shouldn't I be willing to receive gifts from other believers who are listening to that same Savior?"

My shoulders slump as I think of the many times someone has kindly said to me "God told me to give this to you" and my inward response was *Really?*

It's not enough to look grateful—to smile and nod and say nice things. It's the attitude of the heart that concerns the Lord. When our appreciation is sincere, then saying "thank you" to a person is also saying "thank You" to our heavenly Father. "Now, our God, we give you thanks, and praise your glorious name."[35]

Kelly enters through a different door and ends up in the same spot: "God is pleased to receive our praise, our thanks, and our worship. If the God of the universe can receive, so can we."

Penelope learned the hard way how to receive, which is often the best way and sometimes the only way. "A few months ago Father God told me that people were going to start giving me things and that all I was supposed to say in response was 'Thank you.' He didn't want to hear 'Oh, you shouldn't have!' or 'It's too much!' or 'Thank you for the thought, but I really can't accept this.' Just 'Thank you.' Shortly after that, I started receiving gifts. It was hard! But to be able to receive freely—knowing the gifts were from God—and just to say a heartfelt 'thank you' was more of a blessing than I could ever have imagined."

THE BIG TEST

God is an exceptional teacher. His lessons are practical, and His tests are open book. After I had spent months studying His Word on the subject as well as soaking up our sisters' words about receiving gifts with a measure of grace, God sent me to North Carolina for my midterm exam.

I was speaking at a women's conference that weekend with lots of time for meeting our sisters in Christ and swapping stories at the book table. I stepped up to speak on Friday night, and my watch promptly fell off when the beaded wristband came to pieces. I held up the sad remains, giving us all a good laugh, then jumped into my message.

Saturday morning I found a small bag waiting for me on the podium. Not one, but *three* new watches were tucked inside, each a different color! No way could I refuse them, standing in front of hundreds of smiling women. I was so flabbergasted I put on all three at once, feeling my cheeks flush with an equal measure of delight and embarrassment.

Lord, how can I accept such a gift?

His answer was swift and sure. *Just think of Me when you wear them.*

I would, absolutely. *But, Lord, don't I need to thank someone for being so generous?*

You have, Liz. It was My idea.

The truth of His Word began to sink in. "Every good and perfect gift is from above . . ." Gift giving isn't so much *people* being generous as it is *God* being generous through His people.

Unsure how else to handle things, I thanked all 564 women and the Lord before moving on to my message.

Little did I know my test wasn't finished yet.

An hour later I sat at the book table, chatting up everyone who stopped by. When one woman bent down to hug me, I teased, "If you stand up slowly enough, I can steal that gorgeous scarf you're wearing." I was kidding, of course. She knew that, right?

Before I could say another word, she'd wrapped the scarf around my shoulders. "Take it," she insisted. "I've had it for years but never wore it until today. It's meant to be yours."

Stunned, I smoothed my hand over the beautiful silk. What could I say? "Thank you" seemed the right way to go, though it was hard to say with a lump in my throat.

Lord, was this Your idea as well?

Apparently so. The woman was positively gleeful. No way was I going to spoil her fun by handing back her beautiful gift, however much I wanted to. *Smile, Liz. Just smile.*

I should have learned my lesson by this point in the weekend, but the Lord had one more hurdle waiting for me. When the committee met for our closing luncheon, I noticed a silvery mesh necklace one of the women was wearing and told her how pretty it was. Honest, that was *all I said.*

Minutes later I was seated at the table when someone came up behind me and slipped a necklace over my head, her cool hands brushing my chin. "Oh *no!*" I said, turning around to protest, but the Lord quickly overrode me. *Relax. Receive. Be grateful.*

I *was* grateful. Also astounded, overwhelmed, and deeply humbled.

"I want you to have it, Liz," she said as if reading my addled mind. "It blesses me to see you wearing it."

In all my years of speaking, I'd never experienced such a spontaneous outpouring. God was clearly at work. Through their generosity I was (finally) learning how to receive with joy. I also wear their gifts often, thinking of the Lord's kindness and theirs, even as I remind myself, "Freely you have received; freely give."[36]

Sheba already understood how to give and receive in a queenly manner. Now it was time for her difficult test: bidding King Solomon farewell.

I cannot tarry in Jerusalem a moment longer.

At my signal Dabir, my camel master, will lead the first beast toward the gate, and the rest will follow. Their herding instinct will not let them do otherwise.

Tarub stands by my litter, beckoning me with her smile. She has promised to fill my ears with entertaining stories, though what I prefer is a quiet journey home so I may reflect on all I have seen and heard.

The words of Solomon's father press on my heart: "You are my God. Hear, LORD, my cry for mercy."[1] It seems that I may pray to Him at any hour, from any place, and know that I am heard.

Solomon crosses the courtyard now, the golden threads in his robe catching the last rays of sunlight. He snaps his fingers, and a young servant leaps forward, bearing a dish covered with dates, plump with honey.

In a gentle voice he says, "Wisdom is like honey for you."[2]

He knows me well, this king.

Solomon gestures toward the fruit. "Taste and see that the LORD is good."[3] We each choose one and bite into the succulent fruit together. A last shared meal.

Then Solomon says what a king must say, and I answer as a queen must answer. His advisors and mine hover nearby, voicing their approval. Our mission is accomplished, our time here, completed.

I offer a final bow, tamping down my emotions and all that I might say. *I will miss you, Solomon. I will miss your company, your wisdom, your love for our God. I shall not soon forget the kindness in your eyes or the warmth of your smile.*

All at once a deep longing to see my homeland overcomes me. I turn toward the caravan as Solomon's parting words sweeten the air like incense. "Blessed are those who find wisdom."[4]

I nod but do not turn back.

My throne is waiting.

Sheba

Ten

It's
Good
to
End Well

Then she left and returned with her
retinue to her own country.

1 KINGS 10:13

Sheba not only left Jerusalem. She also left her former way of life, her old gods, her old beliefs so she could learn how to "put on the new self, created to be like God in true righteousness and holiness."[5]

But how did Sheba do that, exactly? More to the point, how do *we* let go of our old lives—full of disbelief, distrust, disobedience—and embrace a new life that honors God?

The answer is the same, whether we're talking Sheba's time or the apostle Paul's era or our generation: "Do not conform to the pattern of this world, but be transformed by the renewing of your mind."[6] That's our Sheba. Her mind was transformed by the Word of God flowing through Solomon.

Her entire journey was orchestrated by the Holy Spirit. Sheba didn't travel to Jerusalem to be changed, but she was. Solomon didn't know he would witness the conversion of a foreign queen, yet he did. In fact, he unwittingly prayed for such a thing to happen not long before Sheba arrived.

Ooh! This is beyond thrilling.

AT THE KING'S INVITATION

When Solomon stood before the altar of the Lord to dedicate the temple, he spread out his hands toward heaven and prayed, "As for the foreigner who does not belong to your people Israel but has come from a distant land be-cause of your name . . ."[7]

Hold it. That would include Sheba, yes? She specifically came to see Solomon because of "his relationship to the LORD."[8] She was *exactly* the kind of person Solomon was praying for without knowing it.

Getting chills here.

Solomon's entreaty continued: "When they come and pray toward this temple, then hear from heaven, your dwelling place."[9] Wow. Solomon was asking God to listen to foreign visitors who were not His people yet willingly prayed to Him.

Foreigners. Gentiles. Like our Sheba. Like us.

Are you getting how *big* this is?

Solomon continued, "Do whatever the foreigner asks of you, so that all the peoples of the earth may know your name and fear you."[10] Sister, I am shouting some serious hallelujahs right here. Solomon asked God to expand His blessings over people other than the Israelites (astounding). And to what end? So that all the peoples of the earth would *know His name* and *fear Him.*

Which brings us to Solomon's life verse, as it were, and the heart of his calling as the spiritual leader of Israel: "The fear of the LORD is the begin-ning of wisdom."[11] His book of Proverbs contains "the fear of the LORD" ten times, with another dozen or more appearances in the book of Psalms—his boyhood hymnal, so to speak. And some of those psalms may also be Solo-mon's words, since the songs he wrote "numbered a thousand and five."[12]

Here we are, three thousand years later, learning anew what it means to fear the Lord, all because God opened that door through His anointed king and because a chosen queen responded to His invitation. Oh, the infinite wisdom of our mighty God, whose ways are higher than ours and whose thoughts soar above the highest heavens.

Did Sheba have any inkling that the Lord would use her faith to redeem her people one day? Though the biblical account doesn't mention her taking Solomon's wisdom home in any physical way, it would be perfectly logical and historically typical for Sheba to have her official recorder copy some of Solomon's wise sayings onto clay tablets or papyrus. We can be certain she carried Solomon's wisdom in her heart, where God continued His transforming work in the years that followed.

HOMEWARD BOUND

Once Sheba found what she came for, it was time to retrace her steps back home.

Then she left . . . *1 Kings 10:13*

We have no record of Sheba leaving anything behind other than her gifts for the king. No scandalous accounts, no swift marriages, no secret babies. She simply "turned" (ASV) toward home, "satisfied" (MSG) that her mission was accomplished.

Sheba's destination remained the same; it was her *destiny* that had changed. Though she looked the same on the outside, inside she was a woman reborn. "The old has gone, the new is here!"[13]

. . . and returned with her retinue . . . *1 Kings 10:13*

"She returned home, filled with the knowledge of God."[14] And that big crowd of "servants" (ASV), "officials" (CEV), and "attendants" (EXB)? Their task on the long journey south was to protect and serve their queen as well as guard the long line of camels, weighed down with Solomon's gold and other gifts.

Since we're given no description of their arduous trip, those months must have unfolded without notable incident. At last her palace at Ma'rib came into view.

Home.

. . . to her own country. *1 Kings 10:13*

Whether I've been gone for a few hours or a few days, I am one happy woman when I pull into our driveway. Sheba surely felt the same way when she reached "her homeland" (CEB).

In Solomon's words, "Like cold water to a weary soul is good news from a distant land."[15] You know her people couldn't wait to hear all the news from Jerusalem. But Sheba brought them far more than royal reports and trivial gossip. She shared how her thirst for wisdom was now being quenched by the one true God.

THE PRAISE NEVER ENDS

I wish I could offer more details of Sheba's work among her people, but it's simply not included in Scripture. This we do know: Sheba's commitment to the Lord bore long-lasting fruit. Centuries after Sheba's reign, Isaiah prophesied that someday, when God's kingdom is on earth, "all from Sheba will come, bearing gold and incense and proclaiming the praise of the LORD."[16]

That last phrase tells the glorious tale. It means our queen, our sister, our role model, our Sheba returned to her people and taught them about the God of Israel. Yes, she did. When her people come into His kingdom, they'll be praising His name!

Here's what makes that prophecy from Isaiah even more amazing: modern Yemen is almost entirely Muslim now that the country's once-sizable Jewish population has emigrated. For all the people from the land of Sheba to one day praise the Lord will require a mighty work of redemption only God can accomplish.

I love Matthew Henry's description of that distant day: "The camels and dromedaries that bring gold and incense . . . those of Midian and Sheba, shall bring the richest commodities of their country, not to trade with, but to honour God with, and not in small quantities, but camel-loads of them."[17]

Camel-loads of faith. Camel-loads of praise.

All because Sheba and her camels went first.

Could the same be said about us someday? That we turned to our families, neighbors, coworkers, and friends and shared the truth of a life-changing God? That our example inspired whole communities to serve the Lord and praise His name?

Just the thought of it makes me cry out to Him. *Please, Lord. Let it be so.*

The people of Sheba might well have said of their queen, "She speaks with wisdom, and faithful instruction is on her tongue."[18] Sheba understood what it took to communicate her faith. Wisdom in, wisdom out. Truth in, truth out. It's the same for us, beloved. When His Word goes deep into our hearts, His Word spills easily from our lips.

That's why we're studying Scripture together. If we want to be utterly changed—and change our world in the process—the Bible is the place to begin, for an ending that truly honors God.

ALL'S WELL THAT ENDS WELL

The reported last words of Queen Elizabeth I remind us how quickly life slips through our fingers: "All my possessions for a moment of time."[19]

But time can't be bought. It can only be spent. When you come to the end of your days, what will you be glad you invested your life in?

The king of Israel should have asked that question. Unfortunately, "as Solomon grew old, his wives turned his heart after other gods, and his heart was not fully devoted to the LORD his God."[20] What a tragic end. Only his commendable work on the temple "saved him from being reckoned by the sages as one of the impious kings."[21]

The queen of Sheba, on the other hand, finished exceedingly well: she found the wisdom of God and shared it with her people. Of all her many fine qualities, that's what makes her a worthy mentor, for our generation and for every generation.

Here's what finishing well means to women from every corner of the world. You might find your own voice here. Or wisdom from another sister who speaks your language. Let God's Word and their love for Him wash over you like a cleansing shower of grace.

FINISHING WELL MEANS LIVING WELL

Brenda defines living well as "loving everyone to the best of your ability and forgiving quickly." Loving? We're all in. Forgiving? Harder but so worth it. For many of us our only hope is to throw ourselves on God's mercy and ask His grace to flow through us, untainted by our judgment or anger or disappointment. When God forgives, it's a finished work.

Julia believes ending well means "living now for then, with ever-increasing obedience." I love the idea of living today with the end in mind, but . . . um . . . I have a hard time getting excited about the word *obedience*. Feels kind of Old Testament to me. Law instead of love. Then the Lord showed me "This is love: that we walk in obedience to his commands."[22]

Okay, so no getting around obedience. If we want to end well, it's the key. We could think of obedience as honoring God or blessing God or pleasing God, because it does all three. Honestly? Loving God is all the motivation I need.

Diane is focused on "growing in love for God and participating in what He's doing." Those are the very things His Word encourages us to do: "Live a life worthy of the Lord and please him in every way."[23]

FINISHING WELL MEANS
FINISHING THE RACE

Solomon stumbled before he reached the finish line. Even with God's bless-ing at birth, even with a father who loved the Almighty, "Solomon did evil in the eyes of the LORD."[24] Not very wise for a man full of wisdom. God told Solomon He would tear his kingdom away from him when he died and give the land to one of his servants.[25] Imagine *that* hanging over your head for the rest of your days.

Jenn has a much better plan. She's determined to "finish the course re-gardless of the hardships, detours, or setbacks." Michelle wants to end "with the same enthusiasm, passion, and joy I started with." And Darlene plans on "finishing strong!"

That was the apostle Paul's plan as well: "I have fought the good fight, I have finished the race, I have kept the faith."[26] When we meet such saints, they inspire us to stay the course. Tammy shares, "I had the honor of being with my mother in her last few hours of life. When I asked if she was in pain, she spoke her last words: 'Oh no, honey. I'm fine.' And she *was* fine. She completed the race the Lord placed in front of her."

Please, Lord, may we say the same when it's our turn.

FINISHING WELL MEANS
KNOWING GOD IS IN CONTROL

The way Debbie Jo sees it, "With Jesus in control, you can't help but end well." And Charity reminds us, "His will is always the best ending." Sarah looks forward to "finally seeing what God was working toward." For Stepha-nie, peace is knowing "the results are in the Lord's hands."

In the nineties Twila Paris sang "God Is in Control." That catchy refrain still flits through my mind anytime I'm tempted to doubt, pout, fret, or for-get the One who knows my first breath and my last. As His Word proclaims,

"How great you are, Sovereign LORD! There is no one like you, and there is no God but you."[27]

"God knows the end of the story," Susan reminds us. And Eileen takes comfort in realizing "each step of my life, I was exactly where I was supposed to be."

FINISHING WELL MEANS GIVING GOD THE GLORY

This verse is etched on many of our hearts: "Whatever you do, whether in word or deed, do it all in the name of the Lord Jesus."[28]

Terri wants "an ending that displays the Lord's goodness, majesty, love." For Tracy, finishing well means "knowing that I honored God in all things." And Kellie wants to be sure "that I made my Savior proud. That Jesus was glorified in my life, even if just a little."

I'm thinking of Bill's *Soli Deo Gloria* letters stretched across the wall of his office. We all need a daily reminder that glorifying God, not self, is what makes life worthwhile.

FINISHING WELL MEANS LEAVING A LEGACY

Dee Ann asked the funeral director in her small town what "finishing well" meant to him. He pointed out the door and said, "A long, long line."

Ever considered what people might say at your funeral? Karen hopes those who know her best "can say they saw Christ's love and perfection through my brokenness and imperfections." Brenda believes, "I will have ended well if the three souls who were entrusted to me know Christ as their Lord and Savior." For Amber ending well "means that others were lifted up, encouraged, and added to the kingdom, and I have fulfilled God's plans for me."

That's the legacy Solomon's father left in his wake: "Now when David had served God's purpose in his own generation, he fell asleep; he was buried with his ancestors."[29] So right. To leave a legacy for future generations, we must first serve our own generation.

FINISHING WELL MEANS NO REGRETS

Is it possible to finish without regretting anything you've done? You bet: "Godly sorrow brings repentance that leads to salvation and leaves no regret."[30]

"Having no regret," says Margaret, "is knowing any sins you committed are totally forgiven." That's good news today, tomorrow, and the last day.

Amber defines having no regret as "being able to accept myself and my life for all it is and was—the good, the bad, and the ugly. Ending well is knowing that I didn't have to be perfect to be loved, because I have been perfectly loved the whole time."

Perfectly loved. Perfectly forgiven.

FINISHING WELL MEANS
REMAINING FAITHFUL

Many women said that when they step into heaven, they're eager to hear "Well done, good and faithful servant!"[31] Every word is a rich reward. *Well?* Wonderful. *Done?* Hooray. *Good?* Only because of God. *Faithful?* That's His doing too. *Servant?* What an honor.

Tes shares, "When I think of ending well, I think of my papa. He loved the Lord—walked the walk and talked the talk. And he lived and loved like Jesus until he took his last breath."

Stacey's looking forward to ending "with more faith than when I started!" That's just what God has in mind for us, "because your faith is growing more and more, and the love all of you have for one another is increasing."[32]

FINISHING WELL MEANS ANTICIPATING HEAVEN

Mary, Queen of Scots said it best: "In my end is my beginning."[33] For Sheba and for all of us who believe in the saving grace of God, the finish of one life is merely the start of another. Rather than our lives ending, we simply step into a new realm.

Laurie gently challenged me, "What ending? Eternity awaits!" Gotta love that kind of thinking. Vickie knows the end of this life "will be just the beginning of the plans God has for us!" Mary cannot wait to "meet our Lord face to face," and Paula will be grateful to "finally be in the arms of my Jesus."

Yes, yes, yes, on all the above.

Jean gives us a glimpse of heaven when she writes, "As my dad was dying, he saw tears in my eyes and said, 'Why are you crying? Death isn't bad. I see both sides now. I see the other side. I'm okay.'"

"Rest in peace" is a cliché, but that's really what we're after. Peace with God, peace with others, peace with ourselves. We seldom get to choose our last words, but if I could, I'd love to speak a benediction over anyone who might be there: "Grace and peace be yours in abundance."[34]

FINISHING WELL MEANS STARTING TODAY

Doris gets the credit for this one: "Today is a good place to begin finishing well."

That's part of the legacy the queen of Sheba passes on to us. This "bold and forward-thinking"[35] woman was all about making the most of each day. She studied, she pursued, she asked, she listened, she marveled, she spoke truth, she encouraged, she learned, and in the end she praised the Lord and urged others to join her.

We know women like that. We want to be women like that.

She is clothed with strength and dignity;
> she can laugh at the days to come.[36]

Yes, that kind of woman. A queen in our own realm, however large or small. Even so, it's His kingdom that draws our focus. Someday we'll lay our crowns before His throne and say, "You are worthy, our Lord and God, to receive glory and honor and power, for you created all things, and by your will they were created and have their being."[37]

So worthy, Lord. More than our words can ever say.

FINISHING WELL MEANS ENDING WITH BEAUTY

Ruthie wrote, "Ending well does not mean everything tied up with a pretty little bow. But it does mean ending with beauty."

On the last Sunday in January, my mother-in-law turned eighty-six. This was what we'd prayed for: that she would live long enough to celebrate her birthday. Though honestly, *celebrate* wasn't quite the word for it.

Mary Lee Higgs was dying. All of us could see it. The frailness of her body, the shallowness of her breath. No appetite, little thirst. It's heartbreaking to watch someone endure that level of pain.

The three men she loved most were in the room—her husband, her only son, her only grandson. And me, the woman who took too many years to realize what a treasure her mother-in-law was. In studying the book of Ruth and learning about Ruth's devotion to Naomi, I'd finally gotten the message a few seasons ago and began showering my mother-in-law with much-deserved love and affection. *Thank You, Lord Jesus.*

As I looked down at my precious Mary Lee, sorrow broke against me in a huge, enveloping wave. The Higgs men, with their tender hearts, stood watching from a bit of a distance, not certain how they might care for her needs.

That's when Beauty slipped into the room.

The love and grace and compassion of Jesus overwhelmed me. I bathed Mary Lee's face and moistened her lips with balm and rubbed lotion into her parched hands. I combed her hair and smoothed my hand lightly over her brow, then took her to the rest room, honoring her privacy, helping where I could. I rearranged her pillows and straightened her bedding and gave her sips of water, then fed her when the aide came by with dinner.

You would have done all those things and more. But care giving doesn't come naturally to me.

My son watched from her bedside, dumbfounded. "Where did you learn this stuff, Mom?"

I told him I'd worked in a nursing home when I was a teenager. But in my heart I knew that wasn't the full story. This wasn't Liz, a trained nurse's aide, doing her duty. This was Beauty making His Presence known.

"This only do I seek: that I may . . . gaze on the beauty of the LORD."[38] He was there in the room. I saw Him in my beautiful mother-in-law's face. She looked so elegant. Her skin was stretched smooth against her cheekbones, her classic nose—one of her best features—long and regal, was silhouetted against the pillow.

We said good-bye that day, thinking we would see our beloved Mary Lee again soon.

When the phone call came five days later, I wept with sorrow, softened only by the memory of spending one last afternoon with her and the assurance that she had just stepped into the arms of her Savior.

I have seen what ending well looks like. It looks glorious. "Your eyes will see the king in his beauty and view a land that stretches afar."[39]

It's
Good
to Be
His

A woman who fears the LORD
is to be praised.

PROVERBS 31:30

I've loved every minute of our journey. If Sheba's story has surprised you, challenged you, inspired you, changed you, then thanks be to God!

Before we knock the last bit of sand from our shoes, here's what the queen of Sheba taught us about becoming His kind of woman:

- **Be bold** and take frequent leaps of faith.
- **Be open** to whatever God has prepared for you.
- **Seek wise counsel** from trustworthy sources.
- **Be humbled,** trusting Him to lift you up.
- **Be honest** with God, with yourself, with others.
- **Encourage everyone** who crosses your path.
- **Praise God** in all things and in every season.
- **Give generously,** with open hands and heart.
- **Receive graciously,** to honor God and the giver.
- **End well** by loving well all the days of your life.

It's not a question of picking and choosing. God provides the courage, strength, and ability to do all these things and more, according to His sovereign will.

Our job, beloved? Hold on tight. It's going to be an amazing ride!

Discussion Questions

If your book club will be chatting about *It's Good to Be Queen* in a single session, here are ten questions to get things rolling. You can also use them to enhance your personal takeaway when you've finished reading the book. In either case, dive in!

1. Sheba showed us her strength of character by embarking on a long, difficult journey in search of wisdom. Is there anyone other than Jesus, living or dead, for whom you would travel some distance in hope of gleaning that person's wisdom? If so, who would that be?

2. Sheba shared with Solomon all that was on her mind. Why do you think she was so open, so vulnerable? And what might have motivated Solomon to listen so intently? Have you ever opened up to a stranger, perhaps while traveling? Or had someone pour out his or her story to you? What was the outcome?

3. Solomon asked God for wisdom yet received abundantly more. What would you like to ask God to bless you with today? How can you be confident that He will honor your request? And how will it change your life when He does?

4. Initially chapter 4 was titled "It's Good to Be Humble"—until I realized Sheba didn't arrive with an attitude of humility. At some level, pride is an issue for all of us. Have you ever been humbled by the Lord, perhaps through another person? How does maintaining a proper view of God help us avoid becoming prideful?

5. Freedom comes when we speak the truth, as Sheba did, putting aside our apprehensions. What fears do you need to overcome in order to be completely honest with God? With others? With yourself? Why is honesty vital to any relationship?

6. If you've taken any kind of personality test, what did you discover about yourself? Is encouraging people one of your natural or spiritual gifts, or is that something you would like God to help you with? What have the encouragers in your life taught you about the most effective ways to encourage others?

7. Once Sheba understood the source of Solomon's wisdom, she praised his God and proclaimed her allegiance to Him as well. What prompts you to praise God, and how do you usually express it? Of all the praiseworthy attributes of God, which one holds the most meaning for you, and why?

8. When you are generous with others, how do you hope they'll respond to your gifts? And how do you handle things if they are less than enthusiastic? What have you learned about gift giving over the years?

9. For some of us, receiving gifts is harder than giving them. Do you prefer to be the giver or the receiver? Why might that be the case? On pages 137–141 I suggest several ways to see receiving in a new light. Which one most speaks to you, and why?

10. To end something well might mean finishing a major project on time or turning to a new chapter in life or preparing to step from this world into the next. How did Sheba's story end well? And what does finishing well mean to you?

Study Guide

This in-depth guide is designed with Bible-study groups in mind. Whether you meet for two sessions, ten sessions, or anything in between, these chapter-by-chapter questions should enrich your Bible-study experience. (No camels needed.)

We're discovering much about Sheba and her place in history. Here we'll explore how God's timeless truths can impact our relationship with Him and with the world. When it comes to studying Scripture, we don't simply want to *know*. We want to *grow*.

As we revisit the journey from Ma'rib to Jerusalem and spend more time with Solomon and Sheba, we'll look for personal, practical ways to apply what we're learning. You'll need a place to write your answers—a notebook, a computer, whatever works—and the willingness to explore God's Word and your story.

What an adventure we have waiting for us!

# CHAPTER 1: **It's Good *to* Be Bold**

Read chapter 1 (pages 3–17).

1. Right from the opening verse of 1 Kings 10, we learn several vital facts about the queen of Sheba. She kept up with international news, knew about King Solomon, and was curious about his God. She was also bold enough to put Solomon's wisdom to the test.

   a. What do you find appealing about Sheba's boldness? If being bold comes naturally to you, how might you use it for advancing God's kingdom? If being bold is a stretch for you, why is it important to make the effort? How does Acts 4:8–13 encourage you?

   b. Sheba's desire for wisdom fueled her long journey north. We know wisdom is different from knowledge. How do Proverbs 2:6, 10; 3:21; and 8:12 make that distinction clear?

   c. On pages 16–17 we considered ways a bold believer can be like a lion. Yet even a lion's strength can give out. What promise do you find in Psalm 34:10, and how could that apply to a situation you're dealing with right now?

2. Sheba's trek across the desert was dangerous, with the threat of wild animals and even wilder weather.

   a. On your spiritual journey, what are some of the challenges you face? Trust issues, perhaps? Fears? Doubts? Family or friends who don't share your faith? How might the words Moses spoke to Israel, recorded in Deuteronomy 31:6, bolster your courage?

   b. Sheba traveled hundreds of miles in search of wisdom. How do Proverbs 4:7; 16:16; and 19:8 spur you to go deeper? And how would putting those words into action impact your daily schedule?

c. Simply learning God's Word isn't our goal; obeying it is. As recorded in Luke 11:28, Jesus said, "Blessed rather are those who hear the word of God and obey it." Day in and day out, how can you move from hearing (reading, studying) to obeying? What motivation does 1 John 2:5–6 offer? And in what ways does obedience require boldness as well as restraint?

3. Here's how some of our online sisters define boldness in their lives.

   Boldness is . . .
   - "being confident enough in Christ that I don't fear rejection."—Ammie
   - "standing in His forgiveness as I share my story of radical grace."—Michelle
   - "facing a conflict head-on and speaking the truth in love."—Karla
   - "claiming God's promises every day for myself and for others."—Mary Kay
   - "realizing the power within me is the same power that raised Christ from the dead!"—Rhonda

   a. Which one of the above definitions most resonates with you, and why?

   b. It's your turn to put into words what boldness means to you.

   c. Now that you've defined it, write out one specific step you will take this week to exercise boldness in living out your faith.

CHAPTER 2: **It's Good *to* Be Open**

Read chapter 2 (pages 21–35).

1. Only in movies is Sheba hailed as "more beautiful than Bathsheba" with eyes "as blue as an aquamarine."[1] That may describe the European actress who played her, but that is not the Queen of the South we find in Scripture.

   a. If you've always imagined the queen of Sheba as beautiful, why is that so? How would it change your opinion of her if she were not at all attractive by the world's standards? What does God call beautiful in each of the following passages: Proverbs 24:3–4; Isaiah 28:5; 52:7; and Mark 14:3–6? How do these truths reshape your definition of *beautiful*? And what insight does Ecclesiastes 3:11 offer?

   b. Esther's year-long beauty treatments are described in Esther 2:12. Take a moment to calculate how many hours and dollars you spend each month on your appearance, from head to toe, haircuts to pedicures. Would you consider redirecting a small portion of that time and money (two hours? twenty dollars?) to something that would make the world a more beautiful place for others? What ministry or organization would provide that opportunity for you?

   c. The Bible offers a few clues to Solomon's appearance and distinctive qualities, outlined on pages 29–30. What would you say is the most defining truth about Solomon? Does it have anything to do with his position, wealth, or appearance? What does 1 Samuel 16:7 say matters most to God?

2. Sheba opened both her mind and her heart to Solomon—a first step toward opening her mind and heart to God. Once again she leads by

example. To help us follow in her footsteps, let's explore the three questions I raised about openness on pages 34–35.

a. *Are you willing* to open your heart, your life to God's leading? If you're hesitant, what might be the reason(s)? Think of a hoped-for outcome that would increase your willingness. What help do you find in these verses: Psalm 28:7; 145:13; and Proverbs 3:5–6?

b. *Are you eager* to know and serve the Lord? In 2 Corinthians 8:11–13 we find a common scenario: eager to get started, not so eager to finish. If follow-through is a challenge for you, what wisdom do you find in Peter's words to the elders in 1 Peter 5:2–3?

c. *Are you available* to go and do what God asks of you? What would happen if you handed Him your calendar? Does that idea delight you? Frighten you? In Psalm 27:4, David expresses his desire to spend all his days in the house of the Lord. How can we manage that kind of intimacy with God yet still do His work beyond church doors?

3. Here are some benefits our sisters have found in sharing their heartfelt thoughts with someone they've not met before and may not see again, rather like it was for Sheba and Solomon.

It's good to be open because . . .
- "giving voice to your troubles lets you see how small they really are."—Kim
- "it's almost like talking to yourself. You hear your words, see a reaction from someone, and then can better judge your situation."—Kathy
- "a stranger is more likely to be honest than a friend or family member, who may just want to make you feel better."—Tina

- "once you put your thoughts into words, they stop chasing around in your head, so you can hear the still, small voice of God again."—Cindy
- "sharing my struggles with a stranger brought me to church, which led to my salvation. Praise God!"—Tammy

a. Which one of the above statements do you most connect with?

b. Now finish the sentence yourself: "It's good to be open because . . ."

c. What is God asking you to be open to right now? Write down both His calling and your commitment to moving forward in a measurable way this week.

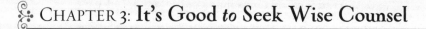

Read chapter 3 (pages 39–50).

1. Seeking direction from the Lord and His Word always comes first. As we read in Psalm 119:24, "Your statutes are my delight; they are my counselors." Seeking wise advice from God's servants is also part of His plan, according to Proverbs 19:20: "Listen to advice and accept discipline, and at the end you will be counted among the wise."

   a. Do you think of yourself as a seeker, in need of further knowledge? Or as a counselor, ready to help others find their way? How is it possible to be both? In 1 Chronicles 28:9 David gives his son explicit directions about seeking the Lord. How could you apply King David's words to your life?

   b. In 1 Kings 3:9 we find Solomon's request for wisdom. What might happen if you made the same request of God? How could Colossians 1:9–10 strengthen your resolve to do so?

   c. If God said, "Tell Me what I should give you," what would be on your list? (Your real list, not your wow-look-what-a-good-person-I-am list.) Would wisdom make your top five? Why or why not? Take a moment to pray—right now—and ask the Lord what He wants you to include on your list of heartfelt desires.

2. God equips trustworthy believers with the necessary wisdom and discernment to guide others, just as He prepared Solomon to answer Sheba's many questions.

   a. I shared how God provided wise counselors before I realized I needed them. If you've had a similar experience, what was the outcome? And what did you learn from it?

b. On pages 45–46 we explored what questions we would ask of God. Now it's your turn: What question(s) would you like God to answer? And how can you be certain He will offer a satisfactory response? Read Psalm 17:6; 38:15; and 91:14–15 for solid assurance.

c. What area of your life would benefit from the input of a wise counselor right now? If you have someone in mind, are you ready to ask him or her? What's holding you back? And what will help you move forward?

3. If you're wondering where to find that godly advisor, here are some recommendations from our sisters around the world.

I seek wise counsel from . . .
- "my husband, who truly has my best interests at heart. He also weighs the impact any decision could have on our family."—Michele
- "a dear mentor, who is grounded in the Word. I go to her when I know there is something I may not want to hear but need to hear."—Amy
- "my pastor. He takes me to God's Word and walks me through what He says to us."—Debrah
- "a licensed counselor, who is able to listen without judgment. Her wise counsel comes from a heavenly source."—Judy
- "my mom, who is full of godly wisdom. Her honesty springs from her deep love for me."—Amy

a. Where do you usually turn for wise counsel?

b. Of the resources mentioned above, which one had you not considered?

c. Whom do you need to reach out to this week for guidance? And what do you need to ask that person? Choose a time and place to make that happen.

Read chapter 4 (pages 53–64).

1. One of our online sisters wrote "Humility is as hard as pride is easy." So right, Cathy. That's why we need God's help to be humbled. It doesn't come naturally to most of us.

   a. Think of someone you know who is genuinely humble, and jot down a few of his or her admirable traits. What do the qualities listed in Colossians 3:12 and Galatians 5:22–23 tell us about the source of this person's humility and where we need to turn as well?

   b. In 1 Peter 5:5 we're directed to clothe ourselves with humility, and Galatians 3:26–27 tells us we have been clothed with Christ. How can we put on humility like a garment?

   c. God assures us in Isaiah 45:23 that before Him "every knee will bow." Have you been humbled in the way Sheba was, overwhelmed by another person's material and spiritual blessings to the point of speechlessness? How might that moment have prepared Sheba's heart for God's grand entrance? What did you gain from your own experience?

2. My story of being humbled in the Dominican Republic was difficult to share because of my foolish pride—the what-will-people-think problem. Maybe you've been down a similar road. The good news? God's opinion is the one that truly matters.

   a. In Psalm 144:3 David marvels, "LORD, what are human beings that you care for them, mere mortals that you think of them?" How does the Lord answer that question elsewhere in His Word? What assurance does He give us again and again? See if 1 John 4:13–16 might help shape your response. How does that truth build your faith?

b. The splendor of Solomon's palace, his banquet, his servants—all were designed to inspire awe. God is preparing a banquet for us, as we learn in Luke 14:15 and again in Revelation 19:9. That magnificent wedding supper is meant to fill us with wonder and humble us until our thoughts are entirely of God and not of ourselves. Write out Exodus 15:11. Then read it aloud with all the reverence His Word deserves.

c. When was the last time you knelt before the Lord—to pray, to repent, to worship? Why does being humbled physically also humble us spiritually? What light does Psalm 95:6–7 shed on the importance of kneeling before God?

3. Here's what some of our sisters have learned about being humbled by the One who loves us.

It's good to be humbled because . . .
- "God taught me that my pride interferes with His working in me and in those He wants to reach through me."—Rebecca
- "it helps me make the heart switch from humiliated (centered on me) to humbled (focused on God)."—Natalie
- "God has a plan for us. Humility allows Him to lead us into that plan."—Laurie
- "I have accepted who I am and my place in this world. I am precious *only* because He loves me."—Jaime
- "humility is birthed at the feet of Jesus."—Vickie

a. Which of their comments rings most true to your experience?

b. How would you finish "It's good to be humbled because . . ."?

c. If you are able to kneel right now, do so. Confess what is weighing on your heart. Listen for His loving response. Then, as a group or individually, acknowledge His greatness: "Yours, Lord, is the greatness and the power and the glory and the majesty and the splendor, for everything in heaven and earth is yours."[2]

CHAPTER 5: It's Good *to* Be Honest

Read chapter 5 (pages 67–79).

1. Sheba's first spoken words show us how bold, open, wise, humble, and honest a woman who seeks after God can be.

   a. Proverbs 24:26 declares, "An honest answer is like a kiss on the lips." How would you elaborate on this unusual comparison? And how could it apply to Sheba's admission to Solomon?

   b. When you need to confess a difficult truth, especially if you're uncertain how others will respond, how do you prepare yourself? Do you pray in advance? Practice what you're going to say? Consider all the ramifications? Have a mental list of excuses ready? Read 1 Kings 10:6–7 again, and note Sheba's style of speaking the truth. What does she do—and not do? How might she serve as a good example?

   c. According to Ephesians 4:15, what's the right way—and the right reason—to speak the truth? Describe a situation when someone's choice of words or tone of voice softened the blow as he or she confronted you with a hard truth. How else can we communicate the truth with genuine compassion instead of judgment?

2. It's good to have a healthy fear of the Lord. But fearing people—and, in particular, their reactions—can keep us from being open and honest with one another.

   a. Of the dozen fears listed on page 73, which one(s) have you wrestled with? In most cases do such fears come to fruition? If and when they do, how could you minimize the damage? What wisdom does Proverbs 29:25 offer?

b. Psalm 59:12 shows us how closely tied are lies and pride. Consider the opposite—honesty and humility. How do they go hand in hand? Is it possible to have one without the other?

c. We discovered a pattern in Scripture: we hear with our ears, we see with our eyes, and then we are changed. Can you trace that progression in your life? When and what did you first hear about God? When did you see the truth about God? And how were you changed?

3. Here's how our sisters define the powerful pairing of honesty with humility.

Honesty with humility means . . .
- "giving up the right to be right and being kind instead."—Nancy
- "seeing my own mistakes so I can forgive the mistakes of others."—Bonnie
- "preferring one another, honoring one another, respecting one another."—Jean
- "putting aside thoughts of embarrassment, pride, and ego and doing what is good, right, and just."—Dot
- "daily dying to myself and allowing Christ to live and love through me."—Rebecca

a. Note the response that speaks the loudest to you.

b. Now finish the sentence yourself. "Honesty with humility means . . ."

c. Think of a situation you are facing right now that would benefit from your honest words delivered with a humble spirit. Then commit to making it happen this week.

CHAPTER 6: **It's Good *to* Encourage Others**

Read chapter 6 (pages 83–94).

1. It takes an exceptional leader to celebrate the wisdom of a peer. Sheba managed that nicely and encouraged Solomon's people as well.

   a. Whether you serve in a leadership capacity for a corporation, a volunteer organization, or the loved ones living under your roof, encouragement is part of your job description. What guidance do Romans 15:1–2 and Ephesians 4:29 provide? On a scale of one to ten, with ten as the high end, how would you rate yourself as an encourager? What would it take to raise your score?

   b. Many women in Scripture are not named and their words not recorded. But Sheba's identity as a queen is well documented, and her public speech is rendered in 1 Kings 10:6–9 and again in 2 Chronicles 9:5–8. From first word to last, Sheba showered her listeners with honest, uplifting, positive words. In what circumstances do you find it challenging to offer encouraging words? What would happen if you made a concerted effort to do so in that setting?

   c. Jealousy and envy can stop the flow of encouragement from our lips. In 1 Corinthians 3:1–5 we learn that spiritual maturity sets us free from such temptations. What wisdom do you find in this passage concerning how we treat those whose perspectives are different from ours?

2. Encouraging people comes naturally to some and supernaturally to others.

   a. What's the difference between a natural gift and a spiritual one? See 1 Corinthians 1:4–9 and 12:4–11 for some clarification. How are spiritual gifts primarily to be used?

b. The call to encourage others isn't only for those with the spiritual gift of encouragement. Turn to 2 Corinthians 13:11 for proof. If the whole church is called to encourage one another, that means saying "Sorry, it's not my gift" isn't an option. How can those who aren't spiritually gifted in this area manage so vital a task?

c. On page 88 we look at the subtle difference between praise and encouragement. When and how did someone offer you genuine encouragement that provided a strong foundation on which you could build?

3. Our online sisters offered some simple but meaningful methods.

To encourage others . . .
- "express confidence in them, giving them an example of a win in their past and saying, 'You'll figure it out. You always do.' "—Cheryl
- "offer a compliment, a kind word, a smile, a hello, a note, a hug."—Valli
- "point out things you see in them that they may not notice or may take for granted."—Heather
- "be sincere. Encourage others when you think of it instead of waiting for a 'better time.' "—Lori
- "listen carefully to hear what they're *not* saying, and lean on the Holy Spirit to give you words that will touch their hearts in a very personal way."—Denise

a. Of these examples which one(s) have you tried, and what were the results?

b. What's your favorite way to encourage others, and why?

c. In your circle of friends and acquaintances, who could use a dose of encouragement? With the Lord's help, how will you reach out to that person this week?

Read chapter 7 (pages 97–111).

1. Psalm 92:1 makes it clear: "It is good to praise the LORD." Sheba and Solomon both excelled at praising Him openly. We can pray in silence and worship in silence, but we generally praise with our voices—speaking, singing, even shouting. As we read in Psalm 109:30, "With my mouth I will greatly extol the LORD."

   a. When, where, and how do you praise God? Privately? Publicly? And what stirs your heart to praise Him? Note the different motivations expressed in Psalm 7:17; 13:6; 16:7; 18:3; 66:20; 68:19; and 72:18. Which one have you experienced recently? How did you express your praise?

   b. According to Psalm 150:6, praising God isn't optional: "Let everything that has breath praise the LORD." When do you find it difficult to praise the Lord? If you've ever praised God simply to be obedient, what did you discover in the process? We know our praises do not change our unchangeable God. How do they change us?

   c. Even God's creation praises Him, as we're taught in Psalm 145:10: "All your works praise you, LORD." Psalm 98:8 describes something marvelous. How might "rivers clap their hands" and "mountains sing . . . for joy"?

2. The first time I watched the queen of Sheba's conversion unfold in Scripture, I was amazed and then overwhelmed at how far she'd traveled to find her Maker.

   a. On pages 99–102 we looked at three truths that assure us Sheba was a child of God. Summarize each truth in a sentence.

Then consider which one you find most convincing, and
explain why.

b. Sheba understood at some level the Lord's eternal love for Israel, which
is described in Genesis 17:7. How might Sheba have grasped this deep
historical and spiritual truth? Reading? Listening? Observing? Or was
it divine revelation? What prompts you to say that?

c. Hebrews 13:15 urges God's people to praise Him without ceasing:
"Through Jesus, therefore, let us continually offer to God a sacrifice
of praise—the fruit of lips that openly profess his name." How was
praising God a sacrifice for the queen of Sheba? When is it a sacrifice
for you to openly profess Him?

3. Psalm 113:2 declares, "Let the name of the LORD be praised, both now
and forevermore." Of all His praiseworthy attributes, here's the one our
sisters cherish most.

I praise God for . . .
- "His indescribable, immeasurable, intentional, unconditional
love!"—Joanie
- "I fail and doubt, yet He still loves me."—Lynne
- "His love. Only by knowing His love can we love others as He
loves us."—Linda
- "He loved me when no one else did. He loved me before I even
knew Him."—Vivian
- "His grace-filled love that says, 'See this girl? She's
Mine.'"—Alison

a. How would you finish the sentence "I praise God for . . ."? Why is that
your favorite of His many glorious qualities?

b. Psalm 113:3 states, "From the rising of the sun to the place where it sets, the name of the LORD is to be praised." It seems we're to praise God every waking minute. Practically speaking, how can we do that?

c. If praising God isn't your default setting—if it isn't something you do automatically—consider how you will incorporate praise into your daily routine this week. Then add it to your calendar.

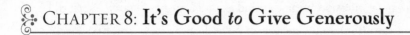

CHAPTER 8: **It's Good *to* Give Generously**

Read chapter 8 (pages 115–124).

1. Though Sheba's extravagant gifts were described at the start of our story, she waited until just before her departure to place them in Solomon's hands.

   a. Parting gifts were the tradition of the time. Why does that make more sense than Sheba's handing them over when she first arrived? In our day, how could saving a hostess gift until we're ready to leave—or even sending a gift after we return home—be meaningful?

   b. Sheba is not the only Spice Girl of the Bible. Read Luke 23:55–56 and Mark 16:1. Who are these three named Spice Girls, and what were their plans for the spices they purchased? Because of the cost of frankincense and myrrh, their gifts required a sizable sacrifice. Although their spices were not put to use that morning at the tomb, were their gifts any less noteworthy? What does that reveal about the value of giving generously?

   c. We meet another Spice Girl in John 12:1–3. Her gift, too, was exceedingly lavish. What do you think motivated Mary of Bethany to be so generous? Continue reading verses 4–8. Why did Judas complain about her gift? And why did Jesus praise it? Since you cannot anoint Jesus's body, as Mary of Bethany did, what else could you offer Him that would truly cost you something?

2. I shared a distressing tale about tossing out a valuable vase I'd been given. As with many of my stories, it was meant to demonstrate human foolishness and celebrate divine forgiveness.

a. Did my confession bring to mind a similar story of yours? What did you learn from your experience? My takeaway (yes, even two dozen years later) is to cherish the giver no matter the gift and to confess the truth no matter the consequences. How does Ephesians 4:25 address this issue? Why might truth be the most generous gift of all?

b. Look around your living room, your kitchen, or wherever you display your favorite possessions. Count all the gifts among them. Do you remember the various gift givers? The special occasions? What are some reasons you keep these presents in view?

c. On page 124 I concluded, "It's not the thought that counts. It's the love that counts." How does 1 John 4:11 capture the heart of gift giving?

3. Giving generously is a good thing. Giving with eternity in mind is even better. Here are some reasons our online sisters love to give.

It's good to give generously because . . .
- "gift giving is an intimate connection, a wordless conversation."—Janet
- "when I give a present, I am giving my heart."—Sarah
- "gifts are as close as I can get to loving people the way Jesus does."—Dori
- "giving helps me get out of myself."—Karrie
- "the Lord has blessed me. How can I not bless others?"—Christine

a. Which of these reasons do you need to embrace?

b. How would you finish this: "It's good to give generously because . . ."?

c. Think of the most generous gift you've ever given. Smile at the
   memory, but don't write it down or share it with anyone in your
   Bible-study group. Instead, thank the Lord for prompting you to give
   that day, and ask Him to provide a clear opportunity for you to be
   generous again this week.

❧ CHAPTER 9: **It's Good** *to* **Receive Graciously**

Read chapter 9 (pages 127–143).

1. I waited until late in our study to explore the common assumption that Solomon and Sheba were lovers. First, so we could meet the real queen of Sheba. Second, so we could understand her growing relationship with God. And third, so we wouldn't be distracted by legends and lore when it's God's Word alone that is our authority.

   a. How do you interpret 1 Kings 10:13: "King Solomon gave the queen of Sheba all she desired"? Do you find evidence in Scripture that their relationship was in any way immoral? Why does human nature take our thoughts down shadowy paths? How can we resist that urge and seek after truth instead of gossip?

   b. I included Ruth and Mary Magdalene as additional examples of biblical women whose reputations have been sullied over the centuries. Can you name others in Scripture? One possibility is Mary of Bethany, whose story has often been confused with that of the sinful woman in Luke 7:36–50. What does Proverbs 22:1 teach us about the value of a reputation? Why is it so important to the Lord that we protect our good names?

   c. What Sheba asked of Solomon was above reproach. What good thing do you want to ask of your King today? You may not be a queen, but you still have a realm of influence. What could God provide that would make you a more effective daughter, sister, wife, mother, leader, worker, neighbor, friend? Write out your request with thanksgiving, and wait with expectation until you can record His certain response.

2. Receiving well is an issue for many of us. Well, for some of us. Okay, for a few of us. If you're willing to admit you start pushing back when a gift is pushed in your direction, it's never too late to learn how to receive more graciously.

    a. In Luke 6:20, Jesus tells his disciples, "Blessed are you who are poor, for yours is the kingdom of God." They'd left everything behind—families, homes, material goods—to follow their Master, so they depended upon the provision and hospitality of others. But, oh, the gift they would one day receive! The Lord's promise is for us as well. How does our willingness to receive from others prepare us to receive God's abundant gift of eternal life?

    b. On page 139 we find Wendy's "five great reasons to receive with gladness and gratitude." Look them over, and then consider which one most applies to you. Do you need to hear from God? Be healed by God? Be invited by God? Be revived by God? Be rewired by God in order to serve others? With these five possible reasons in mind, plan how you can receive with gratitude the next gift you're offered. Consider telling the gift giver how he or she has ministered to you spiritually, not just materially.

    c. Do you sometimes feel unworthy of a gift? In 2 Thessalonians 1:5 those who were suffering for the gospel were assured "you will be counted worthy of the kingdom of God." Though they probably felt worthless—rejected by their neighbors, persecuted by the authorities—they were important to Paul and the other leaders. Far more to the point, they were loved by God. How would knowing you are valuable to God help you receive more graciously from others? When has God tested your willingness to receive, perhaps in much the way He tested me, and what did you discover?

3. Our online sisters shared an abundance of ideas on receiving. Here are a handful.

> **It's good to receive graciously because . . .**
> - "when you accept kindnesses from others, you serve them."—Rebecca
> - "it's like God loving me and affirming me through them."—Xochi
> - "it helps me overcome fear. When someone gives to me from his or her heart, it's kind of scary because I feel vulnerable to so many emotions."—Karrin
> - "it may take more character to receive cheerfully than to give."—Debi
> - "when we accept a gift, it's like closing a circle."—Jeanne

a. Of these comments, which had you not considered before?

b. How would you finish this statement: "It's good to receive graciously because . . ."?

c. Hebrews 12:28 says, "Since we are receiving a kingdom that cannot be shaken, let us be thankful." Whom do you need to express gratitude to this week? Perhaps someone who recently gave you a gift, which you now realize could have been received more graciously. Choose the best method to reach out to that person—a note, a phone call, an e-mail, face to face—and put your gratitude into words.

CHAPTER 10: **It's Good *to* End Well**

Read chapter 10 (pages 147–160).

1. Despite the plain and simple verse at the head of this chapter—"Then she left and returned with her retinue to her own country"—Sheba's exciting journey had only just begun.

   a. The discovery of Solomon's prayer at the dedication of the temple rocked my world. Solomon didn't know Sheba would someday appear in Jerusalem. But God did. In what ways do stories like this help you grasp the sovereignty of God? How does the wisdom expressed in Ecclesiastes 3:14 and Hebrews 4:13 strengthen your trust in a God who knows all, sees all, and is over all, through all, and in all?

   b. I suggested "The fear of the LORD is the beginning of wisdom" as Solomon's life verse, meaning it best defines his core beliefs, appearing again and again in his writings. If you have a life verse, share it here. If not, which one would you choose, and why?

   c. We know that Solomon's life did not end well spiritually. Does that negate all the good he did for the Lord before his wives turned his heart toward their gods? How does Solomon's life serve as a cautionary tale for all who seek to please God? Despite Solomon's disobedience, are all those proverbs and all those psalms he wrote still the Word of God for the people of God? On what do you base your answer?

2. Sheba spent her days well, seeking and sharing God's wisdom. Her story calls to us across the chasm of time, beckoning us to do the same. As Wisdom herself describes in Proverbs 8:20–21, "I walk in the way of righteousness, along the paths of justice, bestowing a rich inheritance on those who love me and making their treasuries full."

a. What steps do you need to take in the days and weeks ahead to ensure life's journey ends well for you? Are there things you need to do for yourself? Things you need to do for others? How might Psalm 40:8 help shape your plans for the future?

b. A thousand years after her death, Sheba was still being talked about, and by Jesus Himself. Another two thousand years have passed, and we are still examining her life while archaeologists search the desert for more clues about this ancient queen. In comparison, how long do you imagine your legacy will continue? Two generations? Three? How does Psalm 45:17 help you grasp the bigger picture? What comfort do you find in 2 Timothy 4:8? Why will your heavenly crown be even more magnificent than Sheba's jewel-encrusted one?

c. Nothing forces us to consider the brevity of life like watching someone we love step into eternity. If you've had that experience, what did you learn about God's faithfulness? About the promise of heaven? Even when our days are filled with the deepest sorrow, joy waits in the wings. Psalm 23 is often read at funerals and for good reason. Share what these familiar words mean to you: "Surely your goodness and love will follow me all the days of my life, and I will dwell in the house of the LORD forever."

3. When I posted my final question online, our sisters poured out their hearts for our benefit.

Finishing well means . . .
- "not that I was perfect, but that I loved well, and it showed through my actions."—Jennifer
- "knowing that what God has started in me, He has already finished."—Sharika

- "I have been salt and light to my family and friends."—Beverley
- "I've done my best to complete the tasks God put before me."—Susan

a. Which one of these comments could you have written, and why?

b. Now consider what "finishing well" means to you.

c. As Laurie said, "What ending? Eternity awaits!" Commit to one small step you can take in the days ahead that will strengthen your long-range vision and fill your heart with hope.

Heartfelt Thanks

Writing a book has a lot in common with traveling across the Arabian Desert. The journey is long, endless sitting is required, a good deal of coffee is consumed, and there's no escape from the heat of a deadline. Ah, but the lessons learned en route and the time spent in God's Word make every minute worthwhile.

My editorial team was especially patient with this one. Laura Barker, Carol Bartley, Sara Fortenberry, Rebecca Price, and Matthew Higgs—the world doesn't contain enough gold and frankincense to reward your continual support and thoughtful direction from start to finish. And Bill Higgs, bless you for encouraging me, book after book after book.

A special thank-you to Edna and Alvin Lindholm, who shared their Yemen experiences with me, and to my friend Pat Hall for making that connection possible. And Glenna Salsbury, bless you for your feedback and direction regarding Sheba's MBTI profile. She's a rare bird, and so are you!

Big hugs to Karen Sherry for her superb map of the land of Sheba, to Holly Briscoe for her fine proofreading, to Angie Messinger for her superior typesetting skills, to Mark Ford for a Shebalicious cover, and to Lilly Higgs for our heroine's colorful online home, www.itsgoodtobequeen.me.

I'm honored to be partnering with the team at Vi Bella Jewelry (www.vibellajewelry.com) to create uniquely designed, handcrafted jewelry for our Queen of Sheba Crown Jewels, helping lift Haitian sisters from the depths of poverty.

I also owe an enormous debt of gratitude to hundreds of Facebook sisters who generously opened their hearts and offered their insights as I worked on each chapter of the book. Your wisdom rivals that of Solomon and Sheba, dear ones. Thank you *so* much.

And you, my reader and friend? I could never do what I do without you.

Notes

Chapter 1: It's Good to Be Bold

1. Steven Weitzman, *Solomon: The Lure of Wisdom* (New Haven, CT: Yale University Press, 2011), 133.
2. Ann Spangler and Jean E. Syswerda, *Women of the Bible: A One-Year Devotional Study of Women in Scripture* (Grand Rapids: Zondervan, 1999), 208.
3. Paul R. House, *1, 2 Kings,* vol. 8 of *The New American Commentary: An Exegetical and Theological Exposition of Holy Scripture,* ed. E. Ray Clendenen (Nashville: B&H, 1995), 161.
4. Claudia Gold, *Queen, Empress, Concubine: Fifty Women Rulers from the Queen of Sheba to Catherine the Great* (London: Quercus Books, 2009), 30.
5. Naomi Lucks, *Queen of Sheba* (New York: Chelsea House, 2009), 17.
6. Harry St. John Philby, *The Queen of Sheba* (London: Quartet Books, 1981), 28.
7. James 3:13
8. "Christina of Sweden Quotes," ThinkExist.com, http://thinkexist .com/quotation/dignity_is_like_a _perfume-those_who_use_it_are /196682.html.
9. Joyce Hollyday, *Clothed with the Sun: Biblical Women, Social Justice, and Us* (Louisville, KY: Westminster John Knox, 1994), 84.
10. Phineas Camp Headley, *Women of the Bible* (Buffalo, NY: Miller, Orton & Mulligan, 1854), 157.
11. Philby, *The Queen of Sheba,* 27.
12. Weitzman, *Solomon,* xxi.
13. J. M. Myers, "Solomon," in *The Interpreter's Dictionary of the Bible: An Illustrated Encyclopedia,* ed. George Arthur Buttrick (Nashville: Abingdon, 1962), 4:399.
14. Nicholas Clapp, *Sheba: Through the Desert in Search of the Legendary Queen* (New York: Houghton Mifflin, 2001), 300.
15. "Archaeological Sites: Sheba," in *NIV Archaeological Study Bible: An Illustrated Walk Through Biblical History and Culture,* eds. Walter C. Kaiser Jr. and Duane A. Garrett (Grand Rapids: Zondervan, 2005), 498.
16. Flavius Josephus, *The New Complete Works of Josephus,* trans. William Whiston, commentary by Paul L. Maier, rev. and exp. ed. (Grand Rapids: Kregel, 1999), 281.
17. Naomi Lucks, *Queen of Sheba* (New York: Chelsea House, 2009), 24.
18. Weitzman, *Solomon,* 140.
19. Matthew 12:42
20. Lucks, *Queen of Sheba,* 41.
21. Weitzman, *Solomon,* 140.

22. Rosanne Gartner, *Meet the Queen of Sheba: More Dramatic Portraits of Biblical Women* (Valley Forge, PA: Judson, 2001), 29.

23. "Archaeological Sites: Sheba," 498.

24. Harold J. Ockenga, *Women Who Made Bible History* (Grand Rapids: Zondervan, 1962), 137–38.

25. Vicki León, *Uppity Women of Ancient Times* (Berkeley, CA: Conari, 1995), 70.

26. 1 Kings 4:30

27. Colleen L. Reece, *Women of the Bible* (Uhrichsville, OH: Barbour, 1996), 65.

28. 1 Kings 4:31

29. Psalm 66:2

30. 2 Samuel 12:24

31. St. John Simpson, *Queen of Sheba: Legend and Reality* (Santa Ana, CA: Bowers Museum of Cultural Art, 2004), 75.

32. Matthew Henry, *Matthew Henry's Commentary on the Whole Bible* (Peabody, MA: Hendrickson, 1991), 2:489.

33. 1 Kings 4:34

34. Ockenga, *Women Who Made Bible History,* 139.

35. Headley, *Women of the Bible,* 156.

36. Klaus Schippmann, *Ancient South Arabia: From the Queen of Sheba to the Advent of Islam,* trans. Allison Brown (Princeton, NJ: Markus Wiener, 2001), 54.

37. Headley, *Women of the Bible,* 165.

38. Headley, *Women of the Bible,* 151.

39. Clapp, *Sheba,* 277.

40. Margaret E. Sangster, *The Women of the Bible* (New York: Christian Herald, 1911), 161.

41. Clapp, *Sheba,* 277.

42. Lucks, *Queen of Sheba,* 51.

43. "Queen Elizabeth the Queen Mother: Biography," IMDb, www.imdb.com/name/nm0703069/bio.

44. Clapp, *Sheba,* 277.

45. Dorothea Harvey, "Queen of Sheba," in *The Interpreter's Dictionary of the Bible: An Illustrated Encyclopedia,* ed. George Arthur Buttrick (Nashville: Abingdon, 1962), 4:311.

46. John H. Walton, Victor H. Matthews, and Mark W. Chavalas, *The IVP Bible Background Commentary: Old Testament* (Downers Grove, IL: InterVarsity, 2000), 429.

47. Elizabeth George, *Women Who Loved God: A Devotional Walk with the Women of the Bible* (Eugene, OR: Harvest House, 1999), June 25.

48. Headley, *Women of the Bible,* 158.

49. Psalm 33:4

50. Psalm 100:5

51. Ecclesiastes 3:11

52. Deuteronomy 33:27

53. Edith Deen, *All of the Women of the Bible* (New York: Harper & Row, 1955), 120.

54. George, *Women Who Loved God,* June 24.

55. George, *Women Who Loved God,* June 24.

56. Josephus, *Complete Works of Josephus,* 281.

57. Henry, *Matthew Henry's Commentary,* 3:649.

58. *NIV Archaeological Study Bible,* note on Judges 14:12–14.

59. Proverbs 1:1

60. Proverbs 1:5

61. Proverbs 1:6

62. R. D. Patterson and Hermann J. Austel, "1 & 2 Kings," in *The*

Expositor's Bible Commentary, ed.
Frank Gaebelein (Grand Rapids:
Zondervan, 1988), 4:101.

63. Patterson and Austel, "1 & 2 Kings,"
4:101.

64. Walton, Matthews, and Chavalas,
IVP Bible Background Commentary,
430.

65. Carole R. Fontaine, "Queen of
Sheba," in *Women in Scripture: A
Dictionary of Named and Unnamed
Women in the Hebrew Bible, the
Apocryphal/Deuterocanonical Books,
and the New Testament,* ed. Carol
Meyers (New York: Houghton
Mifflin, 2000), 271.

66. Acts 4:29

67. Acts 4:31

68. 2 Corinthians 3:12

69. Proverbs 11:2

70. Proverbs 19:2, NASB

71. Proverbs 18:15, NASB

72. Acts 28:31

73. Claire Ridgway, *The Elizabeth Files:
The Real Truth About Queen
Elizabeth I,* www.elizabethfiles.com
/info/elizabeth-i-an-icon/elizabeth-i
-an-iconic-figure/.

74. Proverbs 28:1

75. Proverbs 20:12

76. "Victoria," The British Monarchy,
www.royal.gov.uk/historyofthe
monarchy/kingsandqueensofthe
unitedkingdom/thehanoverians
/victoria.aspx.

77. Psalm 149:4

Chapter 2: It's Good to Be Open

1. Phineas Camp Headley, *Women
of the Bible* (Buffalo, NY: Miller,
Orton & Mulligan, 1854),
153.

2. Thomas Moore, "The Fire-
Worshippers," in *Poetry of Thomas
Moore,* comp. C. Litton Falkiner
(London: Macmillan, 1903), 134.

3. "Ancient Egypt: Personal Hygiene
and Cosmetics," www.reshafim
.org.il/ad/egypt/timelines/topics
/cosmetics.htm.

4. "Ancient Egypt: Personal Hygiene
and Cosmetics."

5. Henry T. Sell, *Studies of Famous
Bible Women* (New York: Revell,
1925), 61.

6. Larry Frolick, *Ten Thousand
Scorpions: The Search for the
Queen of Sheba's Gold* (Toronto:
McClelland & Stewart, 2002), 227.

7. Headley, *Women of the Bible,* 163.

8. Christopher Hibbert, *Queen Victoria:
A Personal History* (Cambridge, MA:
Da Capo, 2000), 202.

9. Naomi Lucks, *Queen of Sheba* (New
York: Chelsea House, 2009), 14.

10. Lucks, *Queen of Sheba,* 54.

11. Margaret E. Sangster, *The Women of
the Bible* (New York: Christian
Herald, 1911), 163.

12. Nicholas Clapp, *Sheba: Through the
Desert in Search of the Legendary
Queen* (New York: Houghton
Mifflin, 2001), 281.

13. Ann Spangler and Jean E. Syswerda,
*Women of the Bible: A One-Year
Devotional Study of Women in
Scripture* (Grand Rapids:
Zondervan, 1999), 209.

14. Job 1:3

15. R. D. Patterson and Hermann J.
Austel, "1 & 2 Kings," in *The
Expositor's Bible Commentary,* ed.
Frank Gaebelein (Grand Rapids:
Zondervan, 1988), 4:101.

16. Ministry of Oil & Minerals Geological Survey and Mineral Resources Board, "Mining Companies in Yemen," November 2008, 1, www.yemenembassy.org/economic/MiningCompaniesYemen.pdf.

17. Patterson and Austel, "1 & 2 Kings," 4:101.

18. verse 10

19. verse 15

20. Lucks, Queen of Sheba, 87.

21. Khalid Al-Dhababi, "Agate (Aqiq): The Wonderful Secrets of Yemen," Islamic Tourism, May–June 2005, www.islamictourism.com/PDFs/Issue%2017/English/48-50%20Aquiq.pdf.

22. Dorothea Harvey, "The Queen of Sheba," in The Interpreter's Dictionary of the Bible: An Illustrated Encyclopedia, ed. George Arthur Buttrick (Nashville: Abingdon, 1962), 4:311.

23. Micah 1:14

24. 1 Samuel 16:12

25. 2 Samuel 11:2

26. 2 Samuel 12:24

27. 2 Samuel 12:25

28. J. M. Myers, "Solomon," in The Interpreter's Dictionary of the Bible: An Illustrated Encyclopedia, ed. George Arthur Buttrick (Nashville: Abingdon, 1962), 4:399.

29. Steven Weitzman, Solomon: The Lure of Wisdom (New Haven, CT: Yale University Press, 2011), xxi.

30. 1 Kings 1:1

31. 1 Kings 1:30

32. 1 Kings 1:31

33. Luke 12:27

34. Francois Boucher, 20,000 Years of Fashion: The History of Costume and Personal Adornment (New York: Harry N. Abrams, 1987), 58.

35. Boucher, 20,000 Years of Fashion, 58.

36. 1 Kings 11:3

37. 1 Kings 11:2

38. Carole R. Fontaine, "Queen of Sheba," in Women in Scripture: A Dictionary of Named and Unnamed Women in the Hebrew Bible, the Apocryphal/Deuterocanonical Books, and the New Testament, ed. Carol Meyers (New York: Houghton Mifflin, 2000), 271.

39. Barbara Black Koltuv, Solomon and Sheba: Inner Marriage and Individuation (York Beach, ME: Nicolas-Hays, 1993), 83.

40. Jacob Lassner, Demonizing the Queen of Sheba: Boundaries of Gender and Culture in Postbiblical Judaism and Medieval Islam (Chicago: University of Chicago Press, 1993), 164.

41. Koltuv, Solomon and Sheba, 83.

42. Proverbs 27:17

43. Proverbs 22:11

44. 1 Kings 3:3

45. Mary Biggs, ed., Women's Words: The Columbia Book of Quotations by Women (New York: Columbia University Press, 1996), 127.

46. Psalm 119:18

47. Jeremiah 9:20

48. 2 Corinthians 6:13

49. James 1:6

50. 1 Peter 3:13

51. 1 Peter 5:2

52. 1 Chronicles 28:9

53. Philippians 3:12
54. Philippians 3:12

Chapter 3: It's Good to Seek Wise Counsel

1. Matthew Henry, *Matthew Henry's Commentary on the Whole Bible* (Peabody, MA: Hendrickson, 1991), 2:489.
2. Acts 7:47
3. 1 Kings 6:1
4. J. M. Myers, "Solomon," in *The Interpreter's Dictionary of the Bible: An Illustrated Encyclopedia*, ed. George Arthur Buttrick (Nashville: Abingdon, 1962), 4:403.
5. Howard F. Vos, *Nelson's New Illustrated Bible Manners and Customs: How the People of the Bible Really Lived* (Nashville: Thomas Nelson, 1999), 176.
6. 1 Kings 6:1–38
7. Hebrews 9:7
8. 1 Kings 7:1–12
9. Proverbs 8:6
10. Henry, *Matthew Henry's Commentary,* 2:489.
11. Flavius Josephus, *The New Complete Works of Josephus,* trans. William Whiston, commentary by Paul L. Maier, rev. and exp. ed. (Grand Rapids: Kregel, 1999), 281.
12. 1 Kings 3:5
13. 1 Kings 3:6
14. 1 Kings 3:7
15. R. D. Patterson and Hermann J. Austel, "1 & 2 Kings," in *The Expositor's Bible Commentary*, ed. Frank Gaebelein (Grand Rapids: Zondervan, 1988), 4:46.
16. 1 Kings 3:9
17. 1 Kings 3:12
18. 1 Kings 3:13
19. Genesis 31:11
20. Numbers 12:6
21. 1 Kings 4:29
22. Matthew 7:7
23. Paul R. House, *1, 2 Kings,* vol. 8 of *The New American Commentary: An Exegetical and Theological Exposition of Holy Scripture,* ed. E. Ray Clendenen (Nashville: B&H, 1995), 162.
24. Proverbs 27:9
25. "Christmas Broadcast 1991," The British Monarchy, www.royal.gov .uk/ImagesandBroadcasts/The QueensChristmasBroadcasts /ChristmasBroadcasts /ChristmasBroadcast1991.aspx.
26. Henry, *Matthew Henry's Commentary,* 2:489.
27. Steven Weitzman, *Solomon: The Lure of Wisdom* (New Haven, CT: Yale University Press, 2011), 138.
28. Hebrews 10:24
29. Isaiah 9:6
30. Isaiah 55:6

Chapter 4: It's Good to Be Humbled

1. Proverbs 1:7
2. Proverbs 14:27
3. 1 Peter 5:6
4. Psalm 113:5
5. Isaiah 55:9, AMP
6. Matthew Henry, *Matthew Henry's Commentary on the Whole Bible* (Peabody, MA: Hendrickson, 1991), 2:489.
7. Howard F. Vos, *Nelson's New Illustrated Bible Manners and*

Customs: How the People of the Bible Really Lived (Nashville: Thomas Nelson, 1999), 222.

8. John H. Walton, Victor H. Matthews, and Mark W. Chavalas, *The IVP Bible Background Commentary: Old Testament* (Downers Grove, IL: InterVarsity, 2000), 430.

9. 1 Kings 10:21

10. "Palaces in Ancient Israel," Bible Archaeology: Palaces, www.bible -archaeology.info/palaces.htm.

11. Kitty Morse, *A Biblical Feast,* quoted in Naomi Lucks, *Queen of Sheba* (New York: Chelsea House, 2009), 60.

12. Henry, *Matthew Henry's Commentary,* 2:489.

13. Walton, Matthews, and Chavalas, *IVP Bible Background Commentary,* 430.

14. Vos, *Nelson's Bible Manners and Customs,* 222.

15. 1 Kings 10:21

16. 1 Kings 2:19

17. Walton, Matthews, and Chavalas, *IVP Bible Background Commentary,* 430.

18. 1 Kings 4:1–6

19. Vos, *Nelson's Bible Manners and Customs,* 222.

20. F. C. Cook, ed., *Exodus to Esther,* vol. 2 of *Barnes Notes* (Grand Rapids: Baker, 1998), 174.

21. Cook, *Exodus to Esther,* 174.

22. Walton, Matthews, and Chavalas, *IVP Bible Background Commentary,* 430.

23. Cook, *Exodus to Esther,* 174.

24. Henry, *Matthew Henry's Commentary,* 2:489.

25. 1 Kings 9:25

26. Leviticus 1:1–17

27. "5930. olah," Bible Hub, http:// biblehub.com/hebrew/5930.htm.

28. Henry, *Matthew Henry's Commentary,* 2:489.

29. R. D. Patterson and Hermann J. Austel, "1 & 2 Kings," in *The Expositor's Bible Commentary,* ed. Frank Gaebelein (Grand Rapids: Zondervan, 1988), 4:101.

30. Patterson and Austel, "1 & 2 Kings," 4:101.

31. Henry, *Matthew Henry's Commentary,* 2:489.

32. Paul R. House, *1, 2 Kings,* vol. 8 of *The New American Commentary: An Exegetical and Theological Exposition of Holy Scripture,* ed. E. Ray Clendenen (Nashville: B&H, 1995), 162.

33. Philippians 2:8

34. Matthew 23:12

35. John 13:8

36. Hebrews 10:22

Chapter 5: It's Good to Be Honest

1. Proverbs 12:17

2. Proverbs 3:13

3. Luke 6:45

4. Proverbs 16:13

5. Proverbs 20:15

6. Simon Sebag Montefiore, *Jerusalem: The Biography* (New York: Alfred A. Knopf, 2011), 31.

7. R. D. Patterson and Hermann J. Austel, "1 & 2 Kings," in *The Expositor's Bible Commentary,* ed. Frank Gaebelein (Grand Rapids: Zondervan, 1988), 4:101.

8. Steven Weitzman, *Solomon: The Lure of Wisdom* (New Haven, CT: Yale University Press, 2011), 138.

9. Weitzman, *Solomon,* 138.

10. Job 6:25

11. Psalm 103:11–12

12. 1 John 1:8

13. Deuteronomy 32:4

14. Hebrews 4:3

15. 2 Chronicles 16:9

16. 2 Corinthians 12:9

17. 2 Chronicles 7:1

18. 1 Kings 8:12

19. 1 Kings 8:27

20. 1 Corinthians 3:16

21. 1 Kings 10:7, MSG

22. 1 Corinthians 2:9

23. John 4:42

24. Job 42:5

25. Matthew 13:16

26. Matthew Henry, *Matthew Henry's Commentary on the Whole Bible* (Peabody, MA: Hendrickson, 1991), 2:489.

27. Henry, *Matthew Henry's Commentary,* 2:489.

28. Ephesians 3:20

29. Psalm 51:2

30. Philippians 2:3

Chapter 6: It's Good to Encourage Others

1. 1 Kings 4:25

2. 1 Kings 4:20

3. Proverbs 28:2

4. "The 16 MBTI Types," The Myers & Briggs Foundation, www.myers briggs.org/my-mbti-personality-type /mbti-basics/the-16-mbti-types.htm.

5. "The ENTJ or Fieldmarshal—2% of Us," ENTJ Central, http://entjcentral .com/.

6. Hebrews 3:13

7. Proverbs 27:2

8. Ecclesiastes 10:12

9. 1 Kings 2:24

10. Proverbs 16:24

11. Romans 12:8

12. Psalm 10:17

13. 1 Thessalonians 5:11

14. Romans 15:7

15. 1 Kings 21:25

16. Matthew 2:16

17. 1 Samuel 13:13

18. 1 Kings 4:32

19. 2 Chronicles 9:23

20. Psalm 119:89

21. 1 Thessalonians 2:13

Chapter 7: It's Good to Praise God

1. Harold J. Ockenga, *Women Who Made Bible History* (Grand Rapids: Zondervan, 1962), 143.

2. Deuteronomy 32:3

3. Psalm 18:46

4. John 20:28

5. 1 Corinthians 12:3

6. Ephesians 2:8–9

7. Matthew 12:42

8. 1 Thessalonians 4:16

9. Matthew 12:42

10. Matthew 12:42

11. Matthew 23:15

12. Matthew 23:17

13. Matthew 23:27

14. Matthew 23:33

15. 2 Chronicles 9:8

16. 1 Kings 10:9, NIrV

17. Psalm 148:14

18. Hebrews 13:5

19. Ephesians 1:4

20. Psalm 103:4

21. Ephesians 4:32

22. 1 John 4:16

23. Hebrews 4:16

24. Titus 3:7

25. Psalm 27:10, NLT

26. Acts 10:33
27. John 16:33
28. 1 Peter 3:20
29. Psalm 36:5
30. Acts 13:38
31. Hebrews 13:8
32. Job 38:4
33. John 3:19
34. 2 Corinthians 4:6, NCV

Chapter 8: It's Good to Give Generously
1. Proverbs 13:20
2. Proverbs 11:16
3. Footnote on 1 Kings 10:10, ESV
4. Shimshon Ben-Yehoshua, Carole Borowitz, Lumir Ondrej Hanus, "Frankincense, Myrrh, and Balm of Gilead: Ancient Spices of Southern Arabia and Judea," *Horticultural Reviews,* ed. J. Janick (Hoboken, NJ: John Wiley & Sons, 2012), vol. 39, chap. 1, http://media.johnwiley.com.au/product_data/excerpt/89/11180967/1118096789-38.pdf.
5. Proverbs 19:6
6. Psalm 112:5
7. 1 Timothy 6:18

Chapter 9: It's Good to Receive Graciously
1. Proverbs 2:16
2. Naomi Lucks, *Queen of Sheba* (New York: Chelsea House, 2009), 88.
3. Lindsay Hardin Freeman, *Bible Women: All Their Words and Why They Matter* (Cincinnati: Forward Movement, 2014), 233.
4. Lucks, *Queen of Sheba,* 17–18.
5. Lucks, *Queen of Sheba,* 25.
6. Alice Ogden Bellis, *Helpmates, Harlots, and Heroes: Women's Stories in the Hebrew Bible* (Louisville, KY: Westminster John Knox, 1994), 164.
7. Dorothea Harvey, "Queen of Sheba," in *The Interpreter's Dictionary of the Bible: An Illustrated Encyclopedia,* ed. George Arthur Buttrick (Nashville: Abingdon, 1962), 4:312.
8. "2656. chephets," Bible Hub, http://biblehub.com/hebrew/2656.htm.
9. Luke 11:31
10. James Faulkner, *Romances and Intrigues of the Women of the Bible* (New York: Vantage, 1957), 78.
11. 1 Kings 10:13, HCSB
12. 1 Kings 10:2
13. 1 Kings 10:3
14. 1 Kings 10:9
15. 1 Kings 10:13, CEV
16. William Butler Yeats, "Solomon to Sheba," *The Collected Poetry of William Butler Yeats* (Digireads.com, 2011), 97.
17. Sue Richards and Larry Richards, *Every Woman in the Bible* (Nashville: Thomas Nelson, 1999), 135.
18. James 1:5
19. Luke 11:9
20. Isaiah 7:11
21. Zechariah 10:1
22. Matthew 9:38
23. Philippians 4:6
24. Matthew 15:28
25. Matthew 7:11
26. Proverbs 8:35
27. Ephesians 3:20
28. Ephesians 5:20
29. 2 Corinthians 9:7
30. Luke 6:38
31. Ephesians 1:6
32. Ephesians 2:8

33. Proverbs 3:34
34. James 1:17
35. 1 Chronicles 29:13
36. Matthew 10:8

**Chapter 10: It's Good
to End Well**
1. Psalm 140:6
2. Proverbs 24:14
3. Psalm 34:8
4. Proverbs 3:13
5. Ephesians 4:24
6. Romans 12:2
7. 1 Kings 8:41
8. 1 Kings 10:1
9. 1 Kings 8:42–43
10. 1 Kings 8:43
11. Proverbs 9:10
12. 1 Kings 4:32
13. 2 Corinthians 5:17
14. Elizabeth George, *Women Who
Loved God: A Devotional Walk with
the Women of the Bible* (Eugene,
OR: Harvest House, 1999), June 27.
15. Proverbs 25:25
16. Isaiah 60:6
17. Matthew Henry, *Matthew Henry's
Commentary on the Whole Bible*
(Peabody, MA: Hendrickson, 1991),
4:277.
18. Proverbs 31:26
19. "Elizabeth I Quotes," BrainyQuotes
.com, www.brainyquote.com/quotes
/quotes/e/elizabethi133449.html.

20. 1 Kings 11:4
21. Louis Ginzberg, "Solomon," in *From
Joshua to Esther,* vol. 4 of *The
Legends of the Jews* (1909), www
.sacred-texts.com/jud/loj/loj406
.htm.
22. 2 John 1:6
23. Colossians 1:10
24. 1 Kings 11:6
25. 1 Kings 11:11
26. 2 Timothy 4:7
27. 2 Samuel 7:22
28. Colossians 3:17
29. Acts 13:36
30. 2 Corinthians 7:10
31. Matthew 25:21
32. 2 Thessalonians 1:3
33. "Her Own Words," The World of
Mary, Queen of Scots, www.marie
-stuart.co.uk/Mariaregina.htm.
34. 1 Peter 1:2
35. Naomi Lucks, *Queen of Sheba*
(New York: Chelsea House, 2009),
95.
36. Proverbs 31:25
37. Revelation 4:11
38. Psalm 27:4
39. Isaiah 33:17

Study Guide
1. *The Queen of Sheba,* directed by
Pietro Francisci (1951; Italy: Oro
Film Production).
2. 1 Chronicles 29:11

Additional Bible Versions

About the Author

LIZ CURTIS HIGGS is the author of more than thirty books, with 4.5 million copies in print. In her best-selling Bad Girls of the Bible series, Liz breathes new life into ancient tales about the most infamous women in scriptural history, from Eve to Mary Magdalene. Liz's award-winning historical novels, which transport the stories of Rebekah, Leah, Rachel, Dinah, Naomi, and Ruth to eighteenth-century Scotland, also invite readers to view biblical characters in a new light.

A seasoned professional speaker and Bible-study teacher, Liz has toured with Women of Faith, Women of Joy, and Extraordinary Women, plus spoken for seventeen hundred women's conferences in all fifty states of the United States and fourteen foreign countries, including Thailand, Portugal, South Africa, and New Zealand.

On the personal side, Liz is married to Bill Higgs, PhD, who serves as director of operations for her speaking and writing office. Louisville, Kentucky, is home for Liz and Bill, their grown children, and Liz's twin tabby cats, Boaz and Samson.

Follow Liz's weekly Bible-study blog on www.LizCurtisHiggs.com and find her on www.Facebook.com/LizCurtisHiggs, on www.Twitter.com/Liz CurtisHiggs, and on www.Pinterest.com/LizCurtisHiggs.

Learn the Truth about God's Goodness from the Bible's Bad Girls

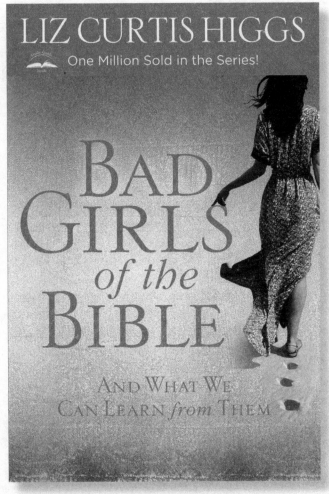

Whether they were Bad to the Bone, Bad for a Moment, or only Bad for a Season but Not Forever, these infamous sisters show women how not to handle the challenges of life. With her trademark humor and heartfelt encouragement, Liz Curtis Higgs teaches readers how to avoid their tragic mistakes and joyfully embrace grace.

Read an excerpt from this book and more at WaterBrookMultnomah.com!

You know Ruth's story.
Now meet her in person.
And prepare to be changed.

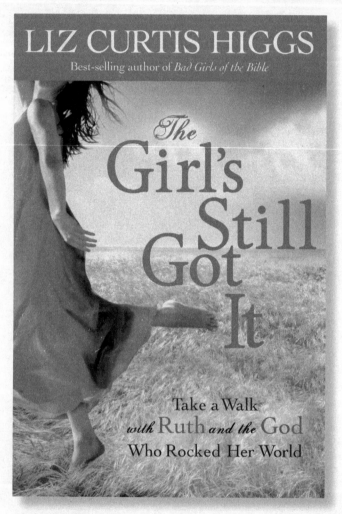

LIZ CURTIS HIGGS
Best-selling author of *Bad Girls of the Bible*

The
Girl's
Still
Got
It

Take a Walk
with Ruth *and the* God
Who Rocked Her World

Think of it as time travel without gimmicks, gizmos, or a DeLorean: a novel
approach to Bible study that leaps from past to present, gleaning timeless truths
that speak to the heart as you experience the day-to-day lives of Ruth, Naomi
and Boaz in a real and intimate way.

Read an excerpt from this book and more at WaterBrookMultnomah.com